The International Library of Sociology

KEY PROBLEMS OF
SOCIOLOGICAL THEORY

Founded by KARL MANNHEIM

The International Library of Sociology

SOCIAL THEORY AND METHODOLOGY
In 22 Volumes

KEY PROBLEMS OF
SOCIOLOGICAL
THEORY

by
JOHN REX

First published in 1961 by
Routledge and Kegan Paul Ltd

Reprinted in 1998 by
Routledge
11 New Fetter Lane, London EC4P 4EE

Printed and bound in Great Britain

British Library Cataloguing in Publication Data
A CIP catalogue record for this book
is available from the British Library

Key Problems of Sociological Theory
ISBN 0-415-17508-9
Social Theory and Methodology: 22 Volumes
ISBN 0-415-17818-5
The International Library of Sociology: 274 Volumes
ISBN 0-415-17838-X

CONTENTS

PREFACE

IN the last few years there have been signs that sociology is becoming an increasingly popular subject in Britain. On the one hand there has been a vastly increased enrolment in universities for courses in sociology as distinct from courses in social work. And on the other there has been an increasing tendency when public issues are being discussed to give weight to the opinions of men calling themselves sociologists. In such a situation it becomes very important that teachers and students of sociology should try to get a clearer idea of the sorts of question which can and cannot be answered in terms of their discipline.

The present book has been written because of the author's sense of the inadequacies of a sociological tradition dominated by empiricism and positivism. The tradition of empiricism leads to attempts to settle public issues by reference to crude ad hoc generalisations. So "right-wing" facts are refuted by "left-wing" facts and vice versa, and in the argument which ensues nothing becomes clear except the value-biasses which the authors seek desperately to conceal. The tradition of positivism on the other hand fails in refusing to interpret observed correlations of fact except in terms of the natural sciences. So the sociologist often appears to have derived little more insight through his precise methods than the untutored layman is able to do through trusting to intuition and common-sense.

The type of scientific approach to sociology which is advocated here is that which emphasises the role of theoretical models in the orientation of the sociologist to his research problems. The attempt to use such models need not, as is sometimes suggested, lead to abstract system building or armchair theorizing. The point is that if we are not explicit about their use, we are likely to use them implicitly in the form of undisclosed hunches in terms of which research data is selected and ordered.

The particular form of model which is advocated is that which is cast in terms of what has come to be called the action frame of reference. This approach was first explicitly advocated by Max Weber and its implications have been drawn out amongst others by Karl Mannheim, Gunnar Myral and Talcott Parsons. It must be stressed, however, that Parsons, in concentrating on the ideal case of a perfectly integrated social system, has ignored some of the crucial methodological issues raised by Weber. In particular it ignores the fact that the necessity of any element of a social relation, institution or system is only a relative necessity and depends upon the extent to which the ends and values achieved by the system are in fact desired by individuals and groups. In emphasising the importance of these ends and values and in recognizing that there may be conflicts and contradictions amongst them, Mannheim and Myrdal have remained more faithful to Weber's own approach.

The point which emerges from this is that, as Weber pointed out, we select problems for sociological investigation because of what he called their "relevance for value". Given that we are concerned with the problem of how particular ends or valued states-of-affairs are to be attained, the sociologist may concern himself with causal or functional investigations to show what institutional arrangements would favour their attainment. But the sociologist, qua sociologist, is in no better position than the layman to say whether or not a particular social end is to be desired. His task as a sociologist is to apply the disciplines of scientific thinking to the discovery of causal relations or the discovery of the relations between social means and ends.

If this is true, we can see a little more clearly what sort of guidance students and the general public may legitimately seek from the sociologist. They may expect him to show the relationship between existing institutional systems and various social ends. They may therefore expect him to expose more sharply the real, as distinct from the utopian, value choices which face them as participants in a particular society. But they should not expect him, nor should he claim, to be competent to make those value choices for them.

It is in this sense, and in this sense alone, that sociology may be thought of as a radical critical discipline. It will simply fall into bad repute if it fails to recognize this and seeks to compensate for the conservative ideological commitments of its recent past by embracing a new political radicalism. On the other hand, if it does recognize its limitations, it will lay the foundations for a more honest and better-informed discussion of value-questions and thus earn a rightful and secure place in the university curriculum.

The line of argument which has been developed in this book is one which I have developed over a number of years as a result of discussions with my teachers and my students, and also in my attempts to relate sociological theory to the understanding of the turbulent time and place in which I first studied it. I shall always be more indebted than I can say to my first teacher, Professor James Irving of Rhodes University, South Africa for opening up the world of social enquiry to me. I also wish to thank Professor Cameron, Mr Peter Alexander and Professor Toulmin for the help they gave me in understanding methodological problems. None of these however bear any responsibility for the line of argument, its weaknesses and blemishes.

I am grateful to Miss Marian Phillipi for help with the index and to Miss Christine Divine, Miss Claire Burton and, above all, to Miss Nora Butterworth for translating my manuscript into a public form. And last, but no means least, I thank my students who, in and out of class, have made the teaching of sociology so satisfying a business for me.

JOHN REX

Leeds University,
February 1961

I

SOCIOLOGY AS A SCIENCE

THE claim of sociology is that the disciplines of scientific argument can be beneficially applied to the study of the relations between men in society. Thus at the outset Comte saw sociology as introducing to the study of social affairs the 'positive' methods which had made great advances in the natural sciences possible. In a different tradition Marx called his socialist analysis of nineteenth century society 'scientific' and contrasted it with other socialist theories which he called 'utopian'. As Durkheim developed his polemic against Comte and Spencer, he argued that their approach was not scientific enough and urged that social facts like natural facts should be treated as 'things'. Pareto argued for the application of 'logico-experimental' methods in sociology. And even Max Weber, who was much the most sensitive of the masters of sociology to the case against a science of society, found it necessary to demand of the proponents of 'understanding' as the appropriate method for history and the social studies, that their arguments should measure up to the canons of scientific proof.

Nor has there been any substantial retreat from this position amongst recent sociologists. Indeed they have been reinforced by such doctrines as logical positivism with its emphasis upon the verification principle, and behaviourism, which remains as a substantial influence in the social sciences, even though some of its more extreme implications may have been abandoned. Thus for example we have the radical neo-positivism of G. A. Lundberg, who contrasts the 'vast amount of trial-and-error blundering and emotional squirmings' of our social adjustments with the relatively systematic adjustments which we make to the

1

physical world, where 'events are immediately referred to their proper place in the framework of science'.[1] So one could go on. A great deal of sociology is written in this crusading spirit, crusading for the application of scientific methods in academic environments, which are often hostile to a science of society for the worst of reasons. One certainly does not want to oppose the spirit which lies behind this crusade. It is true that what Lundberg calls the mental 'hygiene' of scientific method is greatly needed in our thinking, and, not least, in our academic thinking, about society and politics. What needs to be asserted, however, is that the crusade could be more effectively carried on if we devoted a little more time to thinking about what actually is meant by *the* scientific method. All too often our crusaders assume that there is a single and agreed set of principles which we have only to take over from the natural scientists and apply to society. This is a naïve view and it is time that sociologists became better acquainted with the present situation in the philosophy of science, and with the answers of philosophers of science to those who ask them for an account of *the* scientific method.

There was a time when the problem of the philosophy of of science appeared to be that of setting down the principles of inductive logic in such a way that they would bear comparison with the logic of deductive argument. But those days are surely past. What characterizes the philosophy of empirical science today is its increased humility. It is widely recognized that the arguments of empirical science can never have the same sort of certainty as the rational demonstrations of deductive logic do. Science is not thought of as the search for a set of final and absolute truths. Rather it is seen as an always relatively imperfect and incomplete attempt to explain and to predict the events which we experience. And, because this is recognized, the philosophers have abandoned any attempt to legislate to the scientist. Instead they turn to the man whose work has led to relatively successful prediction and adjustment, and ask him what his methods and arguments were, in order to discover which arguments and methods really work. And it is always to be expected that new sorts of argument and method will be found, which may have uses elsewhere.

Thus methodology or the philosophy of empirical science has ceased to be a mainly normative discipline. It has, itself, become

[1] Lundberg, *Foundations of Sociology* (1939), p. 7.

2

empirically oriented. The philosophy of science merges inevitably with the history of empirical investigation. And the philosopher of science must, of necessity be very familiar with the theory and the research methods of the science he is studying.

The situation confronting the methodologist of the social sciences, however, is, in some respects, peculiar. He cannot simply content himself with asking what methods of proved success 'come naturally' to the sociologist, as a philosopher might ask, for example, of the chemist or the biologist. Partly this is because there are so few methods of proved success in sociology. Partly it is because the forms of argument which come most naturally in social discourse are the most misleading. But most of all it is because the great sociologists have all in one way or another disciplined their work by modelling their investigations on those of one or other of the branches of natural science. There is, of course, a great deal to be learned from an analysis of the arguments which have arisen among historians about the interpretation of history, and it is in this field that one can best see the arguments which 'come naturally' to students of society. But even here the most profitable task for the methodologist is the comparative one, that is of comparing the methods used by historians to arrive at their conclusions with those of the scientist. We shall do well to begin, therefore, by considering some of the models of scientific argument which sociologists have drawn from the natural sciences. Our first aim should be to set them out and this will be done in the present chapter. In later chapters we shall be concerned with the actual problems presented to the sociologist by the nature of his subject matter, and by the nature of the questions which he feels called upon to ask. That is to say we shall be concerned with problems of conceptual analysis and sociological theory.

The three major models of scientific investigation which sociologists have taken over from the natural sciences are, firstly, that which sees science as primarily classificatory, secondly, that which sees it as a search for laws, and finally that which sees it as concerned with the establishment of causal relations and sequences. We may now consider each of these in turn, and then go on to consider whether in fact there are not more fundamental aspects of scientific method which underly all of them.

3

SCIENCE AS CLASSIFICATION

The great tradition of thought in the philosophy of science in England since the Reformation has been an empiricist one. Its aims were clearly stated by Francis Bacon in the *Novum Organum*, when he contrasted the methods of empirical science with those of the scholastic thinkers as follows:—

> There are only two ways of searching into and discovering truth. The one flies from senses and particulars to the most general axioms, and from these principles, the truth of which it takes for settled and immoveable, proceeds to judgment and the discovery of middle axioms. And this way is now in fashion. The other derives from the senses and particulars, rising by gradual and unbroken ascent, so that it arrives at the most general axioms last of all. This is the true way, but as yet untried.[1]

This new and 'true' way for empirical science had two possible applications. One was to search for laws by a process of induction by simple enumeration, i.e. by noting the characteristics or behaviour of as large a number of instances of a phenomenon as possible and proceeding to generalize about all instances of that phenomenon. To the question of the validity and the usefulness of this procedure we shall have to return when considering the nature of scientific laws. The second application concerns us more immediately. This was the attempt to describe and to classify the objects in the world which was made by many biologists and natural historians shortly after Bacon's time. In its early stages, biology, with its meticulous observation and description, followed by classification in terms of observable characteristics, seemed to be the empirical science par excellence, the one sphere in which the 'true way' had come gloriously into its own.

Inevitably the drive towards an empiricist method for sociology has led to proposals for the application in sociology of the proved methods of the biological sciences, and no-one has rested his account of sociological method more firmly on the experience of biology than Durkheim. It will be convenient therefore to follow Durkheim in order to understand more fully the implications of the adoption of such a model of scientific method by the sociologist.

[1] Bacon, *Novum Organum* (1878), Book 1.

In *The Rules of Sociological Method*,[1] Durkheim outlines five stages of scientific investigation. These are: (1) Definition of the subject matter in terms of some observable characteristic; (2) Description of normal types after a study of many cases; (3) Classification into species, genera etc.; (4) Comparative and causal investigation of the reasons for variation; (5) The attempt to discover any general law that might emerge in the course of these various stages. Thus in a passage which is striking for its doctrinaire insistence on the one 'true way' for the scientist, Durkheim discusses the question of the economist's study of 'value' as follows: 'If value had been studied as any fact of reality ought to be studied, the economist would indicate first of all, by what characteristics one might recognize the thing so designated, then classify its varieties, investigate by methodical inductions what the causes of its variations are, and finally compare these general results in order to abstract a general formula'.[2] Let us now consider what would be involved in the application of this method in sociology.

Turning to the first stage we find that, in point of fact, it involves two separate tasks. For the indication of the characteristics by which a thing is designated will involve, first of all, the definition of a total field of study, and secondly the definition of the sort of 'thing' which will be found in this field. In the case of biology the field is first of all defined as covering plant and animal life, and then the key characteristics of each species have to be indicated. Unfortunately Durkheim does not distinguish between the two problems involved here and his account of the problems of sociological method is consequently confused.

In any case it will be apparent that both tasks raise difficulties when they are undertaken with regard to social data. Clearly, it is not at all possible to indicate the characteristics by which the sphere of the social is demarcated, with anything like the ease with which the biologist is able to demarcate his field. Nor is it always practical to seek for 'things' in the social world to be classified into species in the way that plants and animals are. For these reasons it may well be impossible even to begin applying biological methods of investigation in all fields of sociology without serious distortion.

It is in fact very difficult to find an empirical characteristic

[1] Durkheim, *The Rules of Sociological Method* (1950).
[2] *Op. cit.*, p. 25.

which might serve to demarcate the social, and Durkheim appears to recognize this in practice, for his own definition of the social involves a complex theoretical concept. Social facts are said to be distinguished by the fact that they are external to the individual and exercise restraint over him. Clearly this definition does not tell us by what empirical characteristics social facts may be recognized, though by confusing the perspective of the scientist with that of the observed participant (who *can* distinguish the social from the non-social in this way) Durkheim gives us the impression that it does. But even he recognizes that it is unsatisfactory, for he goes on to give a second definition of a social fact as, 'every way of acting, which is general throughout a given society, while at the same time existing independently of its individual manifestations'.[1] But this definition is no more satisfactory than the first, for, though in its first part it seems to offer an empirical means of differentiating the social from the non-social, Durkheim would insist that this alone would be an insufficient characterization of the social. Everything therefore turns on the second part of the definition, but here we are faced with a metaphysical conception of little use in actual research.

It must surely be admitted that Durkheim's attempt to provide a purely empirical criterion of the social is a failure. And this is not surprising. For the fact of the matter is that the actual data with which sociology is concerned, and which it seeks to explain, consists of human behaviour and the products of human behaviour, the same data with which psychologists, economists and historians have to deal. The difference lies not in the data, but in the different theoretical frame of reference, in terms of which the data is interpreted. It was Durkheim's great merit as a sociological theorist that he saw and insisted upon the distinctiveness of sociological, as contrasted with psychological explanations. Unfortunately, however, his empiricist bias as a methodologist prevented him from clarifying the true nature of the difference.

There still remains to be considered the possibility of defining in terms of empirical characteristics the various sorts of 'thing' which are to be classified as social species. The difficulty here is that we do not readily experience the social world as being made up of a number of discrete things, each with its own definite spatial boundary, in the way that the biologist does in studying

[1] *Ibid.*, p. 13.

plant and animal life. It seems likely that the real reason why Durkheim insists upon the otherwise rather odd rule that we should consider social facts as things is that he expects sociology to follow a classificatory method, and this method presupposes that the world is experienced in terms of 'things'. If it is not experienced in this way, however, and it proves difficult to conceptualize our experience in these terms, the classificatory method can only be used at the cost of a considerable distortion of experience.

Durkheim's own discussion of the corollaries of saying that social facts are things does not clarify his meaning. He seems primarily concerned to oppose ideological analysis, or, as he says, the tendency 'to focus our consciousness upon, to analyse and combine our ideas' and to insist on the necessity of studying the social world outside our own heads. But this world consists of social relations (whose meaning might well be further analyzed in terms of the goals, aspirations, expectations, understandings and ideas of the related persons) and the real problem is whether a world of this kind can be thought of as consisting of discrete things.

It would seem that it is sometimes possible to think of systems of social relations in this way, but that on other occasions it is more convenient and more illuminating to think of a continuous social process, which could be analysed in terms of its elements, but not in terms of kinds of 'thing'. The 'functionalist' school in social anthropology, in criticizing the misuse of the comparative method, are sometimes insisting on this point (e.g. when they argue that it is not possible to make a comparative study of something like sacrificial customs, because any particular custom loses its meaning when it is torn out of context). The type of work, in which it would seem to be both permissible and useful to regard social facts as things, is in the comparative study of associations and institutions like trade unions, forms of local government, of political parties, or of social processes like political revolutions. This was the sort of work which the Webbs called sociological in Britain, and it is the same approach which characterizes work such as Duverger's recent sociological study of political parties.[1]

It would seem, in fact, that in these fields one is dealing with sets of facts which common-sense is prepared to regard as things,

[1] Duverger, *Political Parties* (1954).

B

quite independently of whether they belong to the realm of the social or not. For this reason the usefulness of the biological type of enquiry in sociology does not depend entirely on our ability to give an empirical criterion for demarcating the social. Common-sense recognizes the existence of certain classes of things and the sociologist can without distortion of the common-sense picture of the world, go on to describe and classify the species.

It should be noted that the 'things' which Durkheim has in mind are 'societies'[1] and that he insists as against Comte that it is possible to study 'societies' rather than simply 'humanity'. He specifically rejects the view of Pascal, of which Comte approves that, 'the entire succession of men, through the whole course of the ages must be regarded as one man, always living and incessantly learning'.[2] But even 'societies' are not the clearly demarcated 'things' which the comparative and classificatory method demands, and only a superficial analysis can make them appear so. To this question it will be necessary to return in later chapters.

For the moment, then, we may accept that it is possible within certain limited spheres to employ the specimen collecting and classificatory methods of the biologist. Granting that this is so, we may now go on to the next stage which Durkheim discusses, namely that of distinguishing the normal specimen from the pathological.

In principle one can imagine this problem as arising in any science, whatever its subject matter, because there is no subject in which instances of what we regard as the same phenomenon do not differ from one another in their detailed appearance; but the problem seems to loom larger in the biological and social sciences for two reasons. Firstly, there probably is more variability among biological and social specimens than is found amongst the phenomena dealt with by the physical sciences, and, secondly, the physicist is sometimes able to avoid the problem by formulating idealized laws, which explain, without claiming to describe, empirical events. The main problem here is now, in the absence of some pre-existing explanatory theory, to write in general terms about a particular class of things or objects. Of course, to some extent the very fact that we are able to name

[1] That is to say, when he comes to discuss the classification of "things" in chapter four of the *Rules*.
[2] Comte, *The Positive Philosophy* (1853), Vol. II, p. 95.

things is an indication that we have some general concept which we attach to the name, but science demands that this general concept should be made explicit and its exact implications defined. This is what the definition of the normal specimen is supposed to do. Durkheim's contention is that the true scientific way of arriving at the concept of the normal is to discover the average of each of the main features of the observed specimens and to construct a type which possesses all these average features. This average type will then be defined for scientific purposes as the normal. For our present purposes we may pass over Durkheim's further contention that this average type may also be used as a criterion of the 'health' of the specimen. The main point is that except in the study of social pathology general sociological statements refer to average (i.e. normal) types.

It is interesting and of some methodological importance at this stage to contrast Durkheim's conception of the average type with the 'ideal' or 'pure' types employed by Max Weber.[1] Durkheim's purpose is primarily descriptive. The average type is discussed, because it is impossible to discuss every empirical instance, and the average is seen as the best method of achieving some measure of generalisation, while at the same time remaining as faithful as possible to the facts. Weber, on the other hand, distinguishes his ideal type sharply from the notion of an average type, and insists that its purpose is not descriptive but explanatory. He also insists that it is a construction of the scientist, rather than something which emerges in a simple way from the facts.

Yet for all this there is some degree of coincidence between the two methodological conceptions. Durkheim's detailed discussion of the average type shows that it is more than merely descriptive. Indeed he actually refers to it as 'the hypothetical being that is constructed by assembling in the same individual the most frequent forms'. And on the other hand Weber insists that ideal types must be formulated in concrete rather than abstract forms, so that they refer to 'objectively possible' courses of action. Moreover, while it is said that the ideal type of meaning must be distinguished from the actual meaning for an empirically existing actor, it is obvious that in practice ideal types will be suggested by actual examples of motivation. In fact, Weber's famous ideal type of the business ethics of early

[1] Weber, *The Methodology of the Social Sciences* (1949), pp. 81–112.

9

capitalism is taken from the papers of Benjamin Franklin, an actual historical figure.[1]

The degree of coincidence or lack of coincidence between these two conceptions of the average and the pure or ideal type illustrates an inherent dilemma facing every empirical scientist. For it is not possible to arrive at 'the most general axioms' by the sort of unbroken ascent which Bacon envisaged. Nor is it possible to make an unbroken *descent* in applying general principles to the explanation of social facts. Durkheim's average type is probably more of a theoretical construction than his empiricism would allow him to admit, and Weber's ideal types are probably less pure than he suggests. Both are concepts which are intended for use at the point at which theory and description confront one another. Without some such concepts a generalizing science of society would be impossible.

The third stage of the process of investigation, which Durkheim proposes should be adopted by sociologists, is the stage which in the biological sciences is the most crucial of all, namely that of classification. Here once again, however, one finds that a purely empiricist approach makes for difficulties. The key problem in making a classification consists in the singling out of a few all-important characteristics, according to the possession of which different species are to be grouped together or separated. But which characteristics are the all-important or, as Durkheim says, the 'essential' ones? How could we possibly know this until we had learned more about the comparative anatomy and physiology of the species? The fact is that unless we have some theoretical hypotheses to work with we should have to proceed by the laborious method of trial and error. For instance if we wanted to classify urban communities we should be faced with a tremendous range of choice among possible bases of classification. Should they be classified according to types of industry, according to the volume of traffic on their roads, according to the ratio of Catholics, Protestants and Unbelievers, or what? The use of a procedure of pure trial and error here might be conceivable, and there were probably times when biologists used such methods. But obviously progress would be more rapid if we said explicitly that at this point some theoretical hypothesis as to which were the most crucial structural features must be put

[1] Weber, *The Protestant Ethic and the Spirit of Capitalism* (1930).

forward. Certainly Durkheim himself employs such a hypothesis at this point, the hypothesis that the crucial differentiating factor between societies is their degree of internal differentiation, which is itself regarded as the consequence of the size of the population and the 'dynamic density' of the society.

Before we go on to the fourth and fifth stages of scientific procedure which Durkheim suggests, we might well ask what further scientific questions remain to be answered when the process of classification is complete. In one sense the answer to this question might simply be 'None'. For classification is itself a comprehensive mode of scientific explanation. It explains by showing the logical relations of one thing to another. Thus the biologist of pre-Darwinian times might easily have been excused if he felt that no further theoretical explanation was necessary. Ultimately the need for explanation stops when our curiosity comes to rest, and, by this psychological criterion, explanation by way of classification might well have seemed sufficient.

Nonetheless in biology Darwin was able to take the further step of showing that the diversity of species which the classifications took for granted could be explained in terms of a further theory, the theory of evolution by natural selection. Thus, from its earliest days sociology was felt to have the duty of going beyond social morphology, in quest of laws of social evolution. Such laws would involve two elements. On the one hand they would seek to describe the order of succession of the social species. On the other they would give an account of the mechanism by means of which one species developed into another. Durkheim's own answers to these questions are given at length in his *The Division of Labour in Society*.[1] There are two main forms of society outlined there, that based on mechanical and that based on organic solidarity. The latter is said to develop out of the former as the size and dynamic density of human society increases. Thus the factor used as a basis for classifying the social species is also used to explain the evolution of society.

In the *Rules of Sociological Method*, however, Durkheim is not solely concerned at this point with the problems of social evolution. He is also concerned with the problems of social physiology, that is with the processes and activities which sustain the structure of the social species. Unhappily he confuses these two

[1] Durkheim, *The Division of Labour in Society* (1949).

questions, and this leads to a most unsatisfactory treatment of the physiological question, without making his views on social evolution any clearer.

On one point, however, Durkheim is clear, and it is of some importance. This is that causal rather than functional studies should have priority in social physiology. As we shall see later there is a widespread tendency among those who see biological and sociological methods as analagous to discuss only the function of social structures and activities, rather than their causes. This is bad for two reasons. On the one hand it imports or appears to import a sort of teleology into scientific explanation, and on the other it tempts the investigator to impute functions to social activities without offering an adequate empirical demonstration. Durkheim has these tendencies in mind when he speaks of those sociologists who 'think they have accounted for a phenomenon once they have shown how they are useful, what role they play, reasoning as if facts existed only from the point of view of this role, and with no other determining cause than the sentiment, clear or confused, of the services they are called to render'.[1]

So much is clear and valuable, but Durkheim's insistence upon the importance of causal studies in the field of sociology is vitiated by his confusion about the nature of the social facts whose causation is to be studied. These facts are not for him, as they are for Radcliffe-Brown, the structure and activities of the parts of the social organism. Rather they are societies as such, and as a result the question of what causal relations hold between activities and structure within the social organism (the problem of social physiology) is ignored as he returns once again to the question of the causes of the emergence of the social species (the problem of social evolution).

The great weakness of Durkheim's book on method lies in his insistence on the classificatory aspects of the biologist's version of scientific method, without going on to give an adequate account of the methods of social physiology. A great deal of important work undertaken by biologists today is concerned with experimental physiology, which has as its object the understanding of the causal relations which hold between the structure and processes in plant and animal organisms. Similar studies are all the more important, albeit on a comparative

[1] Durkheim, *The Rules of Sociological Method*, p. 89.

rather than an experimental basis, in a sociology which at the classificatory stage has only succeeded in classifying social facts into such gross units as 'societies'. It is at this point that Mill's experimental methods, which Durkheim discusses in his chapter on 'Rules for Establishing Sociological Proofs', come into their own. Once again Duverger's *Political Parties* may be recommended as a study in which the logic of these methods is very much to the fore, even though not in the exact form in which it appears in experimental science, as he sets about establishing what is necessary and what accidental in the concurrence of certain structural features of political parties.

Curiously, despite his empiricism, the great weakness of Durkheim's study of method lies in his overeagerness to reach the general formula which is the key to his analysis. Running through all the various phases of his account of scientific procedure, there is a recurring reference to the general theory that the social world consists of social species, having an evolutionary relationship to one another, and that the mechanism which explains the change from one species to the next is to be found in the changing size and dynamic density of a society. This is not a theory which emerges from the facts. It is a general theory which Durkheim takes for granted and which holds his methodology together.

The final stage of sociological enquiry, which Durkheim himself refers to as 'the abstraction of a general formula', should, in fact, only be reached, if we are to adhere strictly to the analogy with biological procedure, after a very careful examination of the comparative anatomy and physiology of the various social species. Moreover it will not be reached simply by 'abstraction'. At this point, undoubtedly, theory is likely to play a more creative role. It must define its own elements and build up from them a model, which explains as economically as possible the diversity of physiology and anatomy exhibited in the social species. It was not to be expected that Durkheim would discover such a formula in the course of a brief essay on method, however, and the fact that he does introduce a general theory serves only to obscure the distinction between the final stages of scientific investigation in the biological manner.

We are now in a position to review the usefulness of the sort of 'biological' approach to sociological investigations which

Durkheim proposes. In the first place we may admit that there are, according to common-sense, 'things' in the social world, which have a clear identity separate from other 'things', and which may be separately described and classified. We may also admit that it is useful in such studies to attempt to formulate an average type, in order, in later studies, to be able to distinguish the markedly pathological. Comparative studies of institutions and associations, or of processes like, say, industrialisation or revolution may all be made in this way. Moreover it is possible to proceed as Durkheim has done, and to classify 'societies' for purposes of comparative study. Beyond this point, however, the insistence upon similarities of procedure between sociology and biology could be unduly restricting and perhaps positively misleading.

It could, for example, in some cases be a highly artificial exercise to divide up history into social species or stages and then ask for an account of the process of evolution from one stage to the next. For social history, if it is properly studied, gives precisely the account of social evolution which we would be seeking. History is not something which we have to guess about from the study of the social species. Rather the species are what we have abstracted from the flux of history. They are extremely useful abstractions, because they do serve to provide reference points for the historian. But to a large extent their order of succession is known and the mechanism which brought them into being is known. It does not require a further law of evolution to explain it. This is not to say that there is no value in the study of social evolution. At a later point we shall discuss the nature of social change. What is objected to is the pretence that we start with things, about the manner of whose evolution we know nothing. This is an artificial attitude forced on us by the analogy with the methods of biology.

A second difficulty arises in the study of 'social physiology'. Clearly, if we do plan to stick close to biological procedures, social physiology must have a central place in our thinking. The great weakness of many who formulate sociological problems in this way, however, is that they have no adequate theory of *social* physiology. Instead of a theory, we are usually offered nothing more than an analogy. The real problem is to indicate what exactly the elements are which constitute a social system or species, and in what ways they interact. This is itself so large

14

a task that it would be difficult to regard it as a mere sub-section of a general sociology. Indeed it may well be that the problems which Durkheim discusses at such great length are really marginal to the main question which usually faces us, namely that of how societies 'work'. And, once this is fully recognized we may well ask whether it is desirable to go on talking about the study of the way societies work as 'social physiology'. It may be the case that another model entirely unlike that of the organism would prove more illuminating. With this question the major part of this book will be concerned.

But the main drawback of Durkheim's biologizing account of sociological method lies in its anti-theoretical bias, which is exhibited by its insistence that social facts must be regarded as 'things', by his empiricist view that type concepts are averages, by his unwillingness to admit that some theoretical hypothesis is necessary before the business of classification can begin and by his failure to outline any 'physiological' theory. The fact is that the very procedures which Durkheim proposes can be profitably followed if theoretical constructions are consciously and deliberately used in the analysis of data. Durkheim himself as we saw, leans upon a general theory. But his reluctance to admit that he is doing so leaves him unable to develop it beyond its barest essentials.

SCIENCE AS THE QUEST FOR LAWS

To Durkheim it appeared natural to regard sociology as the attempt to define, classify and search for the causes of variation of social things. The surprising feature of his work is the absence of any great interest in the discovery of the laws of society, except in the rather shadowy conception of a 'general formula' which is to be abstracted at the end of the process of enquiry. This is the more surprising, because Comte, the founder of the empiricist tradition in which Durkheim stands, looked on the search for laws as the very essence of the positive, as compared with the metaphysical and theological stages of enquiry. Comte gives the following definition of the positive or scientific stage of investigation :—

> In the final, the positive state, the mind has given over the vain search after absolute notions, the origin and destination of the universe and the causes of phenomena and applies itself to the study of their laws, i.e. their invariable relations of succession and

15

resemblance. Reasoning and observation duly combined are the means of this knowledge. What is now understood when we speak of an explanation of facts is simply the establishment of a connection between single phenomena and some general facts, the number of which continually diminishes with the progress of science.[1]

The questions which we have to ask are 'How do we come to have knowledge of the general facts of which Comte speaks?' and 'What methods are involved in the discovery of such facts?' Part of the answer to these questions has already been given, because Comte's approach includes the sort of classificatory methods we have just been discussing. But there is another side to his approach also, represented above by the words 'invariable relations of succession'. When Comte says this, he has in mind, not simply a classificatory science, but science as a system of laws.

Comte does not share Durkheim's anti-theoretical bias. This is clear when he speaks of 'reasoning and observation duly combined'. Our problem could be regarded essentially as a consideration of the part played by 'reasoning' or theory, and that played by observation and description in arriving at the general statements which we call laws.

The extreme empiricist view of this matter is that laws are arrived at by a process of 'induction', and induction is often understood in its simple Baconian form, as induction by simple enumeration. But for all those who implicitly adopt this view, and more adopt it implicitly than would admit to doing so, the so-called 'problem of induction' is bound to arise, because there is no satisfactory way of explaining on an empiricist basis how we can ever make the transition from a sentence beginning 'In all observed cases of X' to one beginning 'In all cases of X'. Here again we encounter the impossibility of Bacon's 'unbroken ascent' from 'the senses and particulars' to 'the most general axioms'.

One thing, however, is clear. The failure of philosophers to solve the 'problem of induction' has not prevented scientists from discovering laws and, what is more, being able to recognize the difference between a law which has been 'established' and other universal propositions which have not. The fact is that the processes of reasoning by which they arrive at these laws are

[1] Comte, *Op. cit.* Vol. I, Chapter I.

16

not those of induction at all. They do not deduce their laws from statements about particular instances. They start with universal propositions as hypotheses, and, when they have tested them by certain agreed tests, regard them as established laws.

The American philosopher Peirce[1] has attempted to point the contrast between the logic which is actually employed in arriving at universal propositions in empirical science with that suggested by the inductive logicians, by setting out the nature of what he calls 'hypothetic' or 'retroductive' reasoning as follows :—

The surprising fact C is observed,
But if A were true, C would follow as a matter of course,
. Therefore there is some reason to suppose that A is true.

And even though such a procedure may appear more scandalous from a logical point of view than inductive logic itself, there is no doubt that Peirce is right. This, in essence, is the form of the reasoning by means of which scientists arrive at *hypotheses* of a universal kind.

The more important point, however, is not how universal propositions as such are arrived at, but how hypotheses become established and recognized as laws. Here the main point to notice is that scientific laws can never be finally verified. If they were, they would not be laws of empirical science. As Kaufmann has pointed out, the first methodological rule of empirical science is that no proposition accepted into the corpus of science is exempt from empirical control[2]. To demand that laws should be finally verified, therefore, would be to demand a rejection of this rule. Laws must not be regarded as finally established truths.

Logical Positivism, which at first sought to set up 'verifiability' as the criterion of a meaningful statement, had some difficulty in explaining the significance of the general laws of science. By the criterion of verifiability they were literally 'nonsense'. When it was admitted that there were other classes of statements than verifiable ones which were necessary both to science and to life, some other category than that of empirical statements had to be found for them, and the tendency was to classify them as imperatives. Thus Schlick says that Laws of

---

[1] Peirce, *Collected Papers*, Vol. 5 (1934), p. 189.
[2] Kaufmann, *The Methodology of Social Science* (1944).

Nature are 'directions, rules of procedure, enabling the investigator to find his way about reality, to discover true propositions, to expect with assurance particular events'.

Popper has insisted against the Positivists that a perfectly adequate criterion of demarcation between scientific and non-scientific statements can be found in the 'falsifiability' of the former.[1] Generally speaking, the more exposed to the possibility of falsification by basic statements a law is, the better it is from a scientific point of view. A law which is regarded as incapable of falsification should not be admitted to science at all. Popper feels that it is a mark of the unscientific character of Freudian and Marxian theory that their exponents regard them as unfalsifiable, or that subsidiary hypotheses are introduced to explain away the failure of theoretical predictions, so that the theories themselves are never challenged at all.

Now it would be extremely useful if we could adopt Popper's criterion of a scientific law, but before doing so there are some reservations which deserve to be mentioned. In the first place we must ask whether in fact all the accepted laws of natural science do conform to this criterion. Even in physics it seems possible that there are accepted laws which do not explain all the facts, but which are accepted because they do enable the physicist to explain the vast majority of them. One cannot imagine a physicist abandoning a theory which has been successful as a basis for predictions over a vast field simply because one experimental observation in a corner of that field appears to contradict it. In such circumstances it would be quite natural for the physicist to adopt one of what Popper calls 'conventionalist stratagems'. And Popper lists these very clearly,

> We may introduce ad hoc hypotheses. Or we may modify the so-called ostensive definitions ... Or we may adopt a sceptical attitude as to the reliability of the experimenter, whose observations, which threaten our system, we may exclude from the science on the ground that they are insufficiently supported, unscientific, or not objective, or even on the ground that the experimenter was a liar.[2]

The difficulty here is that, though such stratagems may be used to keep a theory immune from possible falsification in an indefensible way, there clearly is a case for employing them in the

---

[1] Popper, *The Logic of Scientific Discovery* (1958).
[2] *Op. cit.*, p. 81.

case of very central scientific laws which are challenged by very trivial falsifications. Ultimately this question is a moral one concerning the integrity of the scientist who is left to use his discretion in matters like these.

Another case in which the scientist must exercise his discretion is that in which a basic statement which is falsified is deduced not merely from a general law and certain 'conditions', but from two or more laws and these conditions. In such circumstances it is not clear which of the laws will have been falsified, and, if a controlled experiment is not possible, the scientist may have to judge which of the laws has had most doubt cast upon it. In such circumstances he might come to a decision to retain a particular law, even in the light of falsification of predictions made in terms of it.

None of these reservations, however, need lead us to the view that scientific laws are neither verifiable nor falsifiable. Clearly falsifiability is an important criterion of scientific laws. But it cannot be applied too rigidly. All that we can say definitely is that in the event of widespread and consistent falsifications of the basic statements deduced from them scientists reject general hypotheses, and that by and large an established scientific law is one which has consistently withstood attempts to falsify it. A further point to be noticed is that the rigidity with which the criterion of falsifiability is applied depends upon the stage of development of a science. We should fully expect that in those sciences, whose frame of reference is clear and whose general theories are precisely articulated, falsification of their more important predictions would lead to an alteration of the theory. But there is an earlier stage of development in any science when the scientists are still attempting to create adequate models of a general kind in terms of which their theories can be stated. Such models have great value in that they give the investigator an overall view of his field. Because they have this value, there may be a good case made out for refusing to sacrifice an important general insight because of a few cases which appear as exceptions. This need not lead to dogmatism, provided that the scientist is willing to replace his overall model by a better overall model, if one emerges which is capable of giving a more comprehensive explanation of the facts. Too often the value of general theoretical perspectives is underestimated in the social sciences and the criterion of falsifiability is applied with such

19

rigour that no general theory can emerge, the social scientist being left unable to see the wood for the trees. Instead of bad theories being replaced by better ones, theories as such are rejected before they are properly articulated.

The objection may be put, however, that the difficulty of applying the criterion of falsifiability in the social sciences arises, not from their immaturity, but simply from the fact that social facts are much more variable than are those of the natural sciences. Thus it is sometimes argued that sociological laws must always be relative to a specific culture and that they can never have the universal application which physical laws do. Lundberg has attempted to meet this objection by asserting that the laws of physics do *not* claim to have universal application, but refer to very limited controlled experimental circumstances. When it comes to laws with empirical references, he writes,

'the laws of physics are not only circumscribed in their applicability, they usually describe behaviour which occurs nowhere in the natural uncontrolled universe, but under laboratory conditions such as, for example, in a vacuum, under the assumption of no friction, or under ideal or theoretical conditions. The universality of their practical application flows from the refined measuring instruments that have been devised for measuring the degree to which actual natural situations deviate from the ideal conditions specified in the formal statement of the law. Except for these measurements physics would have to have a separate law for every altitude and every wind velocity. In short every community would have its own laws of physics as it is now sometimes contended that every cultural group must have its own sociological laws. The remedy for the latter situation is clearly the same as has already been applied in the former, namely the selection of social be-haviour phenomena so general as to be present in all cultures (e.g. Le Play's Folk, Work, Place) and deriving from these universal phenomena measures of variation describing in the same basic categories all variations thereof'.[1]

Lundberg then goes on to suggest that there is a parallel bes tween the concept of 'economic man' and the idealised concept-of physics.

Thus Lundberg rejects that idea that greater variability in social data makes the discovery of laws analagous to those of physics impossible and suggests the way in which general models,

[1] Lundberg, *Op. cit.*, p. 140.

such as those we have mentioned, can be replaced by genuine scientific theories. To restate his position in Popper's terms we might say that what is required is that there should be much greater precision about what basic statements can be regarded as falsifying the theory.

The real difficulty, however, arises in connection with the creation of the experimental circumstances necessary for testing idealised sociological laws. It is true that, once a physical law is established experimentally, the exact measurement of uncontrolled circumstances is the means whereby physicists can apply their laws to the prediction of actual events. But Lundberg lays too much stress on the importance of achieving these standards of measurement in sociology, as though the introduction of quantitative methods could, by itself, put sociology on the same footing as physics. The real problem lies in discovering 'social behaviour phenomena so general as to be present in all cultures' and in devising means of testing what is said about such phenomena in their idealised or pure form.

In any case Lundberg is so eager to insist on the absence of any difference in principle between the social and the natural sciences, that he fails to see that the questions which might be answered by the establishment of the sort of laws he has in mind may not be the questions which first gave rise to a science of sociology. The essential problem is to decide on the general concepts in terms of which predictions are to be made about social systems. To Max Weber it appeared that these must be concepts referring to human action, and that, hence, the number of concepts must be as various as the number of possible ends or purposes of action. Weber was interested precisely in those idealised explanations of events which explained a particular culture-pattern. Hence he substituted the notion of 'ideal types' for the notion of universal laws modelled on those of the physical sciences. Other sociologists more recently have returned to the idea of a general system of laws, but the problem is seen as a far more complex one than simply that of selecting universal 'social behaviour phenomena'. At present such work is simply at the stage of conceptual analysis. It is still very far from presenting scientific models, let alone testing them in experimental circumstances.

It would seem, then, that if our standard of the scientific is to be the attainment of a system of empirically falsifiable laws like

those of physics, sociology still falls far short of being a science,
But it is surely absurd to require that every scientific study should
be able to proceed in the way in which physics does in its
maturity. To achieve anything like the status of physics a young
science must first of all begin to develop hypotheses. At the
moment this is just about all that sociologists can do and they do
it on differing levels of generality. There are those whose work is
primarily descriptive, but who, from the study of many cases,
are sometimes able to put forward inductive generalisations.
There are those who, confronting particular sets of research data,
see that such data could be explained by some relatively particularized principle (These are the 'middle principles' which
Robert Merton has suggested should be the main target of contemporary research.[1]) Finally there are those who try to arrive
at ways of seeing the field as a whole, even though they recognize
that much of the work which they are doing is, at the moment,
speculative. The achievement of a system of truly scientific laws
relating to social systems would depend upon the bringing of all
these different levels of study into closer relation to one another.
The aim of this would be the attainment of a comprehensive,
well-established, and falsifiable set of laws. At this stage all that
we can say is that the claim of sociology to be a science rests on
the acceptance of this aim as a long term goal, rather than on
any suggestion that the goal has already been attained.

Clearly then, while the attempt to model sociology on physics
at its present stage of development has led to all sorts of absurd-
ities, it has also led to a careful consideration by sociologists of
the logical nature of general propositions and, with this, to a
more careful analysis of their concepts. Most of the later chapters of this book will, in fact, be concerned with the problems of
conceptual analysis which have arisen in the course of the
attempt to discover the laws of society.

SCIENCE AS THE SEARCH FOR CAUSES

A frequent common-sense conception of science is that it is
simply a quest for the causes of things, and there is no doubt
that the problems which arise for sociologists are frequently
thought of as problems of causation. (e.g. the problem of the
causes of delinquency, or of strikes). Durkheim explicitly calls

[1] Merton, *Social Theory and Social Structure* (1957). Introduction.

for causal analysis when he passes beyond his discussion of classification. And even Weber, whose sociological theory is cast in terms of concepts of action and, in a sense, of motivation (concepts which are often thought of as excluding the notion of causation)—insisted that explanations adequate on the level of meaning should be supplemented by 'causally adequate explanations'.

Now there is a surprising naïvete in this use of the term 'cause', which seems to take little account of the criticism to which the concept has been subjected since the time of Hume and this section will therefore be devoted to a consideration, firstly, of the meaning of the term in scientific, as opposed to common-sense speech, and, secondly to the implications of studies which are based upon the quest for causes in the naïve sense of the term.

What Hume showed was that we could find no justification in our ideas or in our experience for asserting that B was caused by A rather than that B followed A. All that we had to go on from our experience was a repeated temporal uniformity. Yet we do, clearly, mean something more than a mere repeated temporal sequence when we speak of a causal relationship, and it is one of the central tasks of the philosophy of science to explain what this 'more' is that we do mean.

The key to the matter appears to be that we assert that the connection is not merely a repeated temporal one, but that it is, in some sense, necessary. Can we then give any clear meaning to this notion of necessity? The view taken here is that, once we have understood the nature of the relationship between general laws and basic statements reporting empirical events, the meaning of the necessity of a relationship between two events is obvious. When we say that something happened necessarily, rather than accidentally, what we mean is that it was what we would have expected to happen in terms of our deductions from accepted or established laws. Thus when we say that A caused B, rather than merely saying that B followed A, what we mean is that B followed A, *and* that this accorded with our expectations derived from accepted laws.

This view appears to accord with that of Popper who writes,

To give a causal explanation of an event means to deduce a statement which describes it, using as premises of the deduction one or

C

more universal laws, together with certain singular statements, the initial conditions . . .

We have thus two different kinds of statement, both of which are necessary ingredients of a complete causal explanation. They are (1) universal statements, i.e. hypotheses of the character of natural laws, and (2) singular statements, which apply to the specific event in question and which I call the initial conditions. It is from the initial conditions that we deduce the singular statement 'The thread will break'. We call this statement a specific or singular prediction.

The initial conditions describe what is usually called the cause of the event in question . . . And the prediction describes what is usually called the effect.[1]

If this conception of the meaning of causation is correct then it might be applied in sociology as follows: Suppose that we are told that broken homes cause delinquency, what this means is that there is an accepted law asserting a relationship, more or less complex, between broken homes and delinquency and that given the initial condition of a broken home, we should expect delinquency to occur (though, of course, the law here would be a statistical one and the prediction merely a probability statement).

It will be seen that this view of the concept of causation draws attention to the implicit reference of causal statements to laws of a general kind. An alternative reaction to Hume's critique of the concept of causation, which has been adopted by some sociologists, however, is to try to do away with the concept altogether or to replace it by the notion of 'correlation'. The danger of this is that it might lead to an extreme empiricism or to an implicit use of theoretical hypotheses which are not clearly articulated and recognized. As Kaufmann has said,

With Hume's critical analysis of causality in mind, a number of modern philosophers and scientists have suggested that we abandon the use of this term and replace it by 'correlation' or 'function'. While this change in terminology may aid us in avoiding some traditional errors, it may lead, and, indeed has lead to disregard of the highly complex structure of the rules of procedure governing the acceptance and elimination of causal laws. It is apt to suggest statistical investigations without a well-established theoretical basis and over-emphasis on induction by simple enumeration.[2]

[1] Popper, *Op. cit.*, pp. 59–60.
[2] Kaufmann, *Op. cit.*, p. 94.

24

A similar criticism might perhaps be made of those sociologists who refer to Mill's inductive methods as the methodological justification of the sort of causal enquiries which they undertake. It is true, of course, that Mill's methods go far beyond induction by simple enumeration and involve essentially an attempt to falsify laws asserting a uniform relation between antecedent and consequent events. But the great problem in using Mill's methods is always that of deciding which antecedent events are relevant and worth considering as 'causes'. The fact is that most scientists employing Mill's methods find such a criterion of relevance in their own theoretical hunches. The methods are always much more useful if these theoretical hunches are clearly elaborated in the first place and the causal investigation carried on in experimental circumstances, in which irrelevant factors have been eliminated.

The central mistake to be avoided here is that of supposing that Mill has provided us with an alternative to theoretically-directed enquiry. It is true that in a field in which there is no adequate theory we might have to resort to these methods alone, as a trial and error way of finding empirical generalisations of the lowest level. But as soon as middle principles or more general theories begin to take shape in the scientists mind, the methods tend to become an instrument for the testing of theories. Only the most extreme empiricist would imagine that there was some positive merit in showing that he had relied on such methods alone, and thereby excluded theoretical preconceptions.

Thus we must conclude that the continued prevalence of purely causal enquiries in sociology is merely an indication of the extreme immaturity of the discipline, and we should expect that, as more adequate theories are developed, such enquiries will become part of a larger and more systematic plan of enquiry.

CONCLUSION

In this chapter we have considered three separate conceptions of scientific method which have influenced the methodologists of the social sciences. It is not suggested that any one of these is more valuable or important than the others. All in fact have a part to play in the overall plan of scientific enquiry. But one point which emerges clearly in all three cases is the paramount importance of theoretical development going on alongside of description, classification, induction and causal investigation. Directed by theory each of these methods becomes illuminating and profitable. Without its aid a science is likely to remain sterile and planless.

But it is equally obvious that sociology has no general theory of any consequence at the present time. The object of this book is to consider some of the methodological problems involved in the construction of such a theory. When we have discussed them at length it will be possible to return to the problem of scientific proof in sociology.

II

EMPIRICIST SOCIOLOGY

I N the first chapter we were concerned with general method -
ological problems and considered various models of scientific method drawn from the natural sciences. We are now
in a position to consider some of the types of social research
which predominate at present and to consider whether they
could not be more profitably pursued if the sociological investigator had a clearer conception of the subject-matter and the
aim of sociloogical research.

One cannot help being reminded in the consideration of much
contemporary social research of the remark of Merton's to the
effect that most sociologists could be divided into two classes,
firstly those who said, 'I don't know whether what I am saying
is true, but at least it is significant' and, secondly, those who
said 'I don't know whether what I am saying is significant, but
at least it is true'. In this chapter we will be concerned with
sociological research of the second class.

What strikes one at once about most of the social research
which one reads about today is the absence of any clear and
specifically sociological frame of reference guiding the formulation of hypotheses. To a large extent the situation appears to be
very much the same as that of which Durkheim wrote on the
first page of *The Rules of Sociological Method,*

> the designation 'social' is used with little precision. It is currently
> employed for practically all phenomena generally diffused within
> a society, however small their social interest. But, on this basis
> there are, as it were, no human events that may not be called
> social. Each individual drinks, sleeps, eats, reasons; and it is to
> society's interest that these functions should be exercised in an

27

orderly manner. If, then, all these facts are counted as social facts, sociology would have no subject matter exclusively its own, and its domain would be confused with that of biology and psychology.[1]

In the main the problems investigated by sociologists are those which have arisen in the course of philanthropic work or in the struggle for some social reform. In England, for example, there are many who would regard Charles Booth's studies of the incidence of poverty among different groups in London as the main starting point of empirical social investigation in their society. The assumption behind this appears to be that when argument occurs about social reform, the task of the sociologist is to collect the objective facts, as Booth[2], and later, Rowntree[3] did, when they cleared away a lot of the prevailing myths about the causes of poverty. But, however valuable the collection of such information may be from a moral point of view, it is still necessary to ask whether it is at all relevant to sociology, i.e. whether it tells us anything about the nature of 'society', or about the social relations which exist between men.

What exactly is one supposed to learn from such studies? The main point appears to be that there are a certain number of human organisms whose financial resources are such that their chances of biological survival are greatly reduced. Probably no-one would wish to decry the importance of the work of investigators who draw our attention in precise terms to such a fact. But, nonetheless, it is in its essence a biological fact about individual organisms or numbers of individual organisms. It tells us nothing at all about the social relations which exist between the various individuals, either between those on the same income level, or between those on differing income levels. The mere fact of differing income levels does not tell us in what sense those on the same level constitute groups, or whether any such groups can be thought of as constituting a 'class structure'.

It may, however, be argued that work of this kind is sociologically relevant in three ways. Firstly, it may be claimed that the facts of differential income distribution and differential life—chances are themselves important facts about the class-system. Secondly, it may be said that these facts are facts about the

[1] Durkheim, *The Rules of Sociological Method*, p. 1.
[2] Booth, *Life and Labour of the People in London*. (1892–1902).
[3] Rowntree, *Poverty, A Study of Town Life* (1902).

relation between our economic system and family and community life. Thirdly, in showing that the facts were at variance with commonly-accepted myths, the social investigators could claim to have drawn attention to an important set of facts in the sociology of knowledge.

On the first point, our reply would be dependent on our whole conception of the nature of the social. If by the term 'social' we refer to the relations which exist among men then mere facts about the objective characteristics of individuals tell us nothing of any social significance. For the idea of a social relation must surely refer to the expectations which men have of one another, to the meanings which they give to their own and each other's conduct, to the norms governing their behaviour and other facts of a similar order. It is true of course that knowledge of a man's income enables us, if we make certain other assumptions about the meaning of money, to know what he may expect of other people in a market situation. But even here everything depends upon our knowledge of the social significance of money, knowledge which is not provided but, rather, taken for granted by the social investigators. But, in any case, what is usually meant when it is suggested that facts about income distribution are facts about the class system, is that possession of a certain income assigns a man a place, not so much in a market situation as in some sort of status-hierarchy. If this is what is meant, then we must ask that the assumptions about the meaning of income in terms of status-class be made explicit. These assumptions are much less based upon common knowledge than are those about the social significance of money. In general it would seem that if we did have some sociological theory about the nature of social class relations, these facts about income distribution would be highly significant. Standing on their own they are sociologically unrevealing.

The second claim is perhaps more important. The facts of income distribution do provide a vital link in the sociologist's picture of the social system as a whole. It is at this point that the social relations of production and the social relations of consumption are connected. Once again, however, the bare socio-economic facts provide a starting-point only. We should go on, on the one hand, to explore the position in the total system of social relations of production of individuals having incomes of varying sizes, and, on the other, to investigate the pattern of social relations implied by the various family budgets. (These family budgets, incidentally, are by far the most sociologically significant data collected, telling us as they do something of the choices made by individuals in allocating scarce goods to alternative ends).

The third point is rather less important. Any conclusions drawn along these lines depend once again on other knowledge not revealed in the surveys, especially the knowledge of upper-class mythology. Perhaps a great deal of knowledge could have been gained if a proletarian Booth had made a survey of the rich and the two surveys could now be read together!

In each case, however, the essential point to notice is that the sociological significance of the research is thought to lie not in the facts taken by themselves, but in the implications we are supposed to read into them. The difficulty is that these implications are by no means unambiguous. The plea for a more sociologically significant research is not a plea that we should get away from the facts, but that we should attempt to verify some of the propositions which we accept by implication in interpreting the facts (e.g. when it is said that facts such as these are facts about class).

In more recent years social reform has been concerned with a problem with more directly sociological dimensions. This is the problem of social mobility. Inevitably since the extension of the franchise, a demand has developed that occupations carrying the highest prestige and to some extent the highest incomes should be open equally to anyone regardless of the occupation, achievements or income of his parents. Until recently, however, argument about the matter merely took the form of assertion and counter-assertion, supported by the evidence of probably unrepresentative cases. This was an argument, however, which could easily be settled by measurement once sufficient research funds were available, and a number of studies have recently been undertaken both in Europe and America to find out the extent of equality of opportunity in different countries.[1]

Usually such studies have involved two sets of measurements. In the first place it has been necessary to discover the rank order of prestige in which different occupations are placed by popular consent. Secondly, some attempt has been made to discover the frequency with which the children of parents in one occupational

[1] *See* Glass, *Social Mobility in Britain* (1954).

group themselves enter occupations in other occupational groups, or, alternatively, the frequency with which individuals move from one occupational group to another in their own lifetimes.

The facts revealed by the second set of measurements would themselves be interesting to sociologists even if there were no suggestion that the occupations concerned could be arranged in some sort of prestige hierarchy. They would show that an individual in choosing his occupation was subject to some sort of causative factor which continually biased his action in a particular direction rather than being able to choose freely, or randomly. The causal factor might, of course, be a biological one or one due to the physical environment. But our own experience leads us to suppose, prima facie, that amongst the causal factors operating are the actions and expected actions of others which the individual must take into account in planning his own course of action. So studies of occupational mobility do tell us something sociologically important. They tell us about a tendency on the part of parents to advance the chances of their own children entering occupations and to limit the opportunities of the children of others. From the point of view of an individual entering such a society these tendencies to action on the part of others constitute what Durkheim called an external fact or, one might say, a fact about the social structure.

What is added to such studies by the proof that mobility from one occupational group to another is an indication of mobility from one prestige group to another? And what does it mean to say that occupations have differing degrees of prestige? To this there is an immediate empirical and a more theoretical answer. The immediate empirical answer is that the individual in entering an occupation is regarded not merely as one entitled to the rights and duties of his occupational role, but also as one of whom it can be said 'So-and-so has such a degree of prestige'. But the theoretical problems arise when one asks what sorts of behaviour are to be expected from someone who says 'So-and-so has such-and-such a degree of prestige'. What we want to know as sociologists is what new external factor (in the form of the expected behaviour of other individuals) will be placed in the way of the individual of whom such a sentence is spoken.

Of course, the answer to such a question must ultimately be found empirically. We must discover what sorts of behaviour

31

are correlated with saying 'X has X degrees of prestige'. In practice, however, such empirical investigation would involve some preliminary exploration of the concept of prestige, in order to discover what sorts of behaviour were worth investigating. It might, for instance, be worth exploring whether an individual, who is verbally accorded a high degree of prestige by his fellows, was also recognized as entitled to exercize 'legitimate authority' (i.e. to give commands to others which will be obeyed on grounds other than the capacity of the individual to use physical violence) in extra-occupational contexts. In this case the fact that an individual says 'occupation X has X degrees of prestige' would be an indicator of *his* recognition that there were certain very important external or structural facts in his situation.

In fact, what these studies of social mobility indicate quite incidentally is the way in which human beings are constrained in their conduct by the existence of a social environment consisting of the expected actions of their fellows. The main task of sociology should be to describe this social environment. The limitation of the mobility studies from the point of view of any-one interested in general sociology is that they confine themselves to describing a very restricted aspect of this social environment, namely that which is of interest from the practical standpoint of a social reformer. Thus 'enjoying prestige' is taken to be something which is well-understood, and moreover regarded as a good in itself. Interest is then focused on the degree of equality of opportunity in attaining this happy state.

The danger here is that the range of sociological studies should be limited to studies concerned with the administrative problems of a particular society in which there is a large measure of agreement on values. The basic frame-of-reference is thus static. A new and more dynamic approach is introduced if it is recognized that the set of attitudes indicated by the sentence 'Occupation X has X degrees of prestige' is complex *and that it might change*. For instance, it might be that awareness of the existence of a particular prestige scale in the mind of a population would be coupled with an aspiration to alter it. In that case the reversal or destruction of the prestige order might be a more important motive than attaining prestige within it. Once this comparative perspective is introduced, the frame of reference of the mobility studies itself becomes problematic. The new problem which arises is 'Why is it that in this country, mobility within a particular prestige order is desired more strongly than an alteration of the prestige order itself?'

One suspects that the unwillingness to consider this question arises from something more than a desire to get on with one problem at a time. Rather, it involves a value judgement on the part of the sociologists concerned that mobility between prestige classes is more to be desired than any upsetting of the prestige hierarchy. But this in itself will not be regarded as a criticism here. As will be pointed out in later chapters, all selection of research problems involves value judgement, of some kind. The important point is that such value judgement should be made explicit, and that it should not be suggested that these studies are simply bricks in the building up of 'objective' knowledge.

It might be pointed out further, however, that mobility studies might actually distort the truth about the particular social situation to which they refer. By merely asking a sample of individuals to rank occupations in terms of what they believe to be their prestige by popular consent, the studies fail to probe other attitudes of individuals in the sample which may be important. Thus it is perfectly possible that an individual who agrees that a company director is popularly accorded a certain degree of prestige may himself hold that this prestige is not merited. The possibility of such attitudes existing is not even considered in many of the studies which have been undertaken, even though they profoundly affect the sorts of conclusion which are drawn.

The central point to be emphasised here is that the sociologist is concerned with the social determinants of human behaviour i.e. he is concerned to discover the expectations of the conduct of others, of which an individual acting in a social system has to take account in planning his own action. Mobility studies give only a limited and partial account of these determinants. Their main interest is in exposing the degree to which social mobility is attained *given* the existence of certain status-valuations in the minds of the population. It cannot be for a moment supposed that the examination of such studies will ever give us a complete account of existing class and status systems.

Still less can it be supposed that another of the major pre-occupations of contemporary social research will contribute to our knowledge of existing social systems. This is the preoccupation with the statistical study of the causes of various pathological social phenomena such as delinquency. What such studies show is that there are correlations between the occurrence of delinquent behaviour and the occurrence of other physical, biological and social phenomena. This may be very useful from the point of view of the community because alterations in the correlated circumstances might well eliminate undesirable behaviour. But we are not taken very much further in our attempt to understand the social structure, or the social determinants of behaviour. To understand this we would have to understand what expected behaviour on the part of others leads the delinquent to embark on his criminal course. The correlations of the statisticians might suggest the problems here. But they by no means always solve them. Thus if it were shown that there was a correlation between 'broken homes' and delinquency one would still want to know what factors in the behaviour of divorced or separated parents operated as the conditions compelling the child towards delinquency. Of course, in this case the argument is about the degree of detail in which the causative social factors are exhibited, but usually the social findings of the student of social pathology are merged in a much larger body of findings about causative factors of all kinds and the degree to which his researches add to our knowledge of the social structure is small.

In all the cases, thus far mentioned, in fact, since the major focus of interest is social reform of some kind, we find that the additions made to our knowledge of social structure are small. If we are to have even a descriptive account of the specifically social determinants of behaviour, therefore, we should have to turn our attention away from the immediate problems of reform to a much more systematic description of social relations which exist, and of the expectations which individuals have of each other's behaviour when they enter social systems.

One would hope to glean far more of a sociological nature, therefore, from the relatively pedestrian students of social institutions than one would from the social reformers, and it is worthwhile, therefore, to turn at this point to one of the few existing accounts by students in this field of the methods which they have adopted. This is Sidney and Beatrice Webb's *Methods of Social Study*.[1]

[1] Sidney and Beatrice Webb, *Methods of Social Study* (1932).

The Webbs, unlike some of the other empiricist sociologists we have been considering, do appear to realise that the claim to be studying social facts, rather than simply facts of administrative importance, raises certain methodological and epistemological problems. Thus, at the outset, say,

> Let us now consider the nature of the phenomena within the province of sociology. These phenomena are not matter, whether living or non-living, but the relations formed to exist among human beings in their groupings. Such a relation can be known and described as such, irrespective of the human beings whom it concerns, though not without them. A social institution it has been well said 'is a mature, specialized and comparatively rigid part of the social structure.'

Our problem, however, is whether 'relations found to exist among human beings in groupings' can in fact 'be known and described as such, irrespective of the human beings it concerns, though not without them'. The great merit of the sorts of empiricist sociology we have hitherto been discussing is that their conclusions had reference to demonstrable and, indeed, measurable fact. But they were shown to be subject to the criticism that they were not necessarily about the class of facts which should be the sociologists' special concern. The focus of the Webbs' attention on the other hand is the study of social relations. But how far can such social relations be observed and hence how far can verifiable statements be made about them?

We have referred to the specifically sociological field of interest in this chapter variously as covering 'the social determinants of conduct', 'the facts external to the individual as he enters a social system', 'the expectations which one individual has of another's conduct' and so on. These rather cumbersome formulations were used because, unlike the bald term, 'social relations', they do suggest where we have to look for empirical confirmation of our sociological statements. The Webbs, simply, define their field as the study of social relations, a formulation which is eminently satisfactory because it is a notion quite familiar to anyone who has been a human being. But the problem is not merely whether other human beings will understand what we are talking about when we make sociological statements, but whether or not we can offer any sort of empirical proof of what we say.

[1] *Op. cit.*, p. 17.

Inevitably, the Webbs have to deal with this problem. The conclusion which they reach is that 'an institution' is an 'incorporeal and immaterial entity, which in its entirety can neither be seen nor heard, neither tasted nor touched'.[1] But since some sort of sensory contact with the objects of our discourse is essential for sociology, they suggest that the nature of an institution 'in its entirety' must be inferred from its 'partial manifestations'.

Before we go on to consider what these 'partial manifestations' are, it must be noted that the Webbs seem to be committed here to a metaphysical position which would be repugnant to most scientists. The world is thought of as consisting of unobservable entities which are known only by inference from their partial manifestations. A much more acceptable view to most scientists would be that these entities are inventions of the scientist—theoretical entities, the known laws of whose behaviour explains observed phenomena. At least most scientists would be agnostic about the metaphysical question of whether such theoretical entities correspond to unobservable entities in the external world.

This view, however, is one which students of human behaviour find hard to accept. Since everyone in daily life knows what he means by a social relation, it seems artificial to say that such a notion has reference only to a theoretical entity, in terms of which observed phenomena are interpreted. But the reason for this is the peculiar complexity of the epistemological problem of the social sciences. The fact is that social scientists as human beings, as well as the human beings whom they observe, *themselves* continually interpret the behaviour of their fellows in terms of theoretical entities. The trouble is that the sociologist is theoretically interpreting the behaviour of human beings who themselves continually engage in theoretical interpretation of one another's conduct.

To illustrate this with an example. An individual engaged in any particular relationship, say marriage, continually interprets his wife's behaviour as being conditioned by the relation of marriage holding between them. But the sociologist, observing this individual, interprets his conduct towards his wife as being conditioned by this relation and also notes amongst his other behaviour the fact that he believes in the existence of the relation.

[1] *Ibid.*, p. 17.

The danger, here, lies in the fact that the sociologist should take the observed actors belief in the existence of the social relations as proof of its existence. We should, therefore, always be careful to make a threefold distinction between observed behaviour, the theoretical interpretations which observed individuals put on each other's behaviour (we might call these 'participant's theories'), and the theoretical interpretation made by a sociologist of the behaviour of those he observes. If we do not make this distinction, we are in danger of treating as 'fact' entities whose existence has by no means been proved.

The Webbs' 'partial manifestations' prove, in fact, to include elements of all three, and they fail especially to make the necessary distinctions between observed behaviours and participants' theories. Their apparently meticulous analysis of the evidential value of various sources of data is in fact based on rather different distinctions from those which we have made here. It is important, of course, to weight the relative value of documents, literature, interview reports and direct reports of observation. But the crucial distinction is between reports, whatever their form, which record observations in behaviouristic terms and those which purport to talk directly about social relations.

In short, in attempting to describe any social institutions with scientific accuracy it is necessary first to describe exactly the behaviour which is observed and secondly to attempt to discover whether any hypothetical and theoretical model could be constructed, which would enable us to predict the behaviour which we see. The importance of this second stage is that it enables us to give a much more economical account of what we see. The participants' own interpretation of each other's conduct may indeed provide us with useful hypotheses, which we as sociologists might take over as our own to be used in a scientific manner. But they should not be confused either with observed facts or with the sociologist's own theoretical interpretations.

The difference between participants' theories and the sociologist's own lies in the fact that the latter are subject to procedures of verification. If they are true they should be capable of withstanding the non-falsification test in experimental or quasi-experimental circumstances. This, however, presupposes that the theories in terms of which the sociologist interprets behaviour when he talks of 'institutions' will have been or will be subjected to such an independent test. Hence the question arises whether in the purely empirical study of institutions, one by one, as it were, such theories are available. If they are not, should the sociologist confine himself to reporting observed behaviour, since he cannot claim to be doing more than the participants have already done in making largely intuitive interpretations of each others conduct?

This raises the important question of whether purely empirical studies of institutions can claim to be strictly sociological at all. Are they not simply history, using that term in a very narrow sense to refer to an account of what has happened? Or if, out of a desire to avoid being needlessly pedantic, we accept that there is a place for purely descriptive studies in sociology, should we not now ask whether there is not a further task for sociology beyond that of mere description.

In fact it is true that all the studies with which we have hitherto been concerned have been primarily descriptive. How should we proceed beyond this stage? The answer usually given is that we must use the comparative method. But what is the aim of this method? One sometimes feels that those who use the phrase have nothing more in mind than placing a number of cases side by side and then intuitively drawing general conclusions.

The view taken here is that the comparative method is used where the possibility of experiment is absent, in order to show that connections which have been observed to exist between facts, do not exist accidentally, but necessarily. The underlying logic of the comparative method is essentially the same as that of an experiment.

The Webbs, however, are characteristically confused on this issue as are many other social scientists. Although, in one place they seem to grasp the relationship between the comparative and experimental methods, when they say:—

> The limited use that was made of experiment . . . renders indispensable a constant habit of comparing one qualitative observation with another. This accumulation of many observations, though possibly only qualitative or capable of only imperfect measurement may amount to quite effective verification; verification it is true . . . of a low order of probability; such as that on which most of the world's action proceeds.[1]

[1] *Ibid.*, p. 220.

they seem to confuse the problem of proof by the comparative method with two other problems, those of accurate measurement and of reaching adequate generalizations by the method of induction by simple enumeration. Thus they also say:—

> In the learned treatises on logic . . . the author's reference to verification appear principally and indeed usually, to have in view what they seem to regard as the final stage in the method of discovery, namely that of transforming a hypothetical generalization into a demonstrated theory or a law of nature. The more modest sociological investigator does not find himself talking about laws of nature, and he is cautious even about making sweeping generalizations. He realises that his particular science is, at present, far from the stage reached by physics or chemistry, and it stands about where natural history stood in the age of Cuvier and Buffon.[1]

The reference to natural history is indicative of a common empiricist attitude. The implication is that by collecting a number of specimens we will eventually have enough data to give an accurate description. But surely, even the specimen collecting method should lead eventually to the framing of experimental or quasi-experimental questions. At some stage the existence of a particular activity or structural element will appear as problematic, because it occurs in some cases but not in others. Then it will become necessary to conduct experiments or to make systematic comparisons in order to discover what other elements are causally or necessarily related to it.

Once this stage is reached the familiar question arises, 'Which of the other factors present are likely to be the causal ones and therefore worth examination?' Such a question points immediately to the necessity of formulating theoretical hypotheses. Instead of facing up to this, the Webbs retreat into a discussion of the contrast between the qualitative observations of sociology and the exact measurements of the natural sciences.

If it had been recognized in the first place that all attempts to organize the reports of observed behaviour of individuals under the concept of 'institutions' involved theoretical construction this problem could not have emerged in so sharp a form. Far from it being the case that the testing of theoretical hypotheses occurs only at a late stage in the observations of the sociologist, what actually happens is that such hypotheses are being constructed and tested, albeit unconsciously, within what passes as

[1] *Ibid.*, p. 218.

a simple act of observation. The fact is that in trying to discover what sort of social relations exist in an institution we first formulate a hypothesis, either by inference from observed behaviour or from the hints contained in 'participants' theories', and then subject it to possible falsification in 'numerous instances'. The empiricist who pretends to be confining himself to the facts actually ends up by employing unclear theoretical hunches and testing them only in an undisciplined and unsystematic way. The influences of sociological theory lies precisely in the aid which it is able to give in the clearer formulation and testing of these hypotheses.

We are now in a position to draw some conclusions about sociology with an empiricist bias, that is to say about the great bulk of contemporary social research. We have seen that much of it is concerned merely with providing accurate data in the service of social reforms or administration. The emphasis in such studies is on accurate measurement of the phenomena concerned, for it is mistakenly supposed that the use of quantitative methods at this level is the hall-mark of empirical science. The great defect of such research as a contribution to sociology, whatever its usefulness or moral worth, is that it does not differentiate social from other determinants of human behaviour. It is true that these determinants are studied amongst others, but because they are deliberately defined in such a way as to make them easily measureable, their most significant aspects from a sociological point of view are usually ignored. This is particularly clear in studies of social mobility. In order that the extent of transition from one status to another should be easily measurable, the various status groupings have to be defined in the simplest possible way. Hence the aspects of status which are most significant and problematic from a sociological point of view are ignored.

It should not be thought that this criticism is intended as a criticism of operational definitions as such. In the last analysis a science of sociology, like any other science, depends upon empirical confirmation, and this is best obtained by the introduction of operational definitions and measurement. But this is not to say that any data which are presented in quantitative form are significant for the sociologist. What we have to do if we are to obtain quantitative data for sociology, is to begin by constructing some sort of preliminary theoretical model and then devising means of measurement for the relatively complex variables which such a model involves. Sacrificing theoretical clarity for the sake of obtaining easily quantitative data is at least as great a sin for the sociologist as sacrificing accuracy of measurement in order to attain theoretical clarity. Indeed it is a greater one, because if true theoretical clarity is attained, it should be possible to go on to achieve quantitative confirmation of theoretical hypotheses, whereas over-simplified operational definitions may actually prevent the attainment of theoretical clarity.

The other sort of empiricism which has played a large part in sociological research is, as we have seen, the empiricism of the historian and the student of social institutions. Here the principal criticism is not that such writers ignore the sociologically significant data, but that because they underrate the complexity of the methodological problems of verifying sociological statements they tend to treat complex theoretical constructs such as 'social relations' as though they were observable entities. The outcome of this is ultimately an inability to obtain accurate verification of sociological hypotheses. Hence the difficulties in which the Webbs find themselves when they discuss the process of verification. They are forced into arguing that sociology must always be limited to a much lower degree of accuracy in verification than the physical sciences.

Beyond this point we have also suggested that empirical sociology rarely gets beyond the stage of description. If it seeks to do so, it claims to use the comparative method, but because it lacks any sort of theoretical orientation, it is never very clear which are the relevant variables to be compared.

At all points then it would seem that the paramount need in contemporary sociology is for the construction of some sort of provisional models of social relations and social systems. It is not suggested that we should depart entirely from the first and engage in abstract system building. But the first essential is that we should try to discover what it is that sociologists claim their subject is about and having done this to devise means of verifying statements including specifically sociological terms. For this reason the next chapter is devoted to a discussion of the subject matter of sociology.

III

THE SUBJECT MATTER OF SOCIOLOGY

THE dilemma which faces a purely empiricist sociology has emerged in our previous chapter. Either it confines itself to facts which, although they are demonstrable and measurable, are not necessarily *sociological* facts or it talks about social relations and institutions as though they were directly observable entities, and is then forced to admit that its conclusions are vague and uncertain. Is there, then, any way out of this dilemma?

The way out, it is suggested here, is first of all to make a clear differentiation between the social and other determinants of human behaviour, and then to define 'the social' adequately in empirical terms, that is to say to show what sort of statement would count as an empirical verifier of a sociological statement. One sort of empiricist sociology, as we have seen, fails adequately to perform the first task and the other to perform the second. What we wish to emphasise here is that sociological statements (i.e. statements about 'social relations') refer to complex theoretical entities. But this does *not* mean that they are incapable of empirical testing. All science beyond the most rudimentary levels makes reference to such theoretical entities. What it does mean is that some set of rules must be evolved, which will serve to indicate what statements about empirical entities can be regarded as relevant to the verification or falsification of theoretical propositions. The essence of the problem of defining the subject matter of sociology lies in defining what the empirical entities are, which are relevant in this way.

Durkheim was the first of the masters of sociological theory to tackle this problem, and it will be well to begin this discussion by referring to the difficulties which he found in dealing with it.

SOCIAL FACTS DEFINED AS 'EXTERNAL'

Durkheim begins by recognizing clearly that there is a distinct class of specifically social determinants of behaviour. Their specific mark, according to his first formulation in *The Rules of Sociological Method*, is their externality from the point of view of an individual participating in the social system. Thus he writes:— 'When I fulfil my obligation as brother, husband, or citizen, I perform duties which are defined, externally to myself and my acts in law and custom. Even if they conform to my own sentiments and I feel their reality subjectively, such reality is still objective, for I did not create them . . .'[1]

From our own experience of participating in social systems we know well enough what Durkheim means here. Clearly we do differentiate in every-day life between those determinants of our behaviour which come from within us, and those factors indicated by the terms 'obligation' 'contract' 'duty' 'law' and 'custom'. But to say this is not to resolve the further problem of how such facts are to be studied empirically. Is there, in addition to the criterion of social facts as appearing to exercise an external constraint *from the point of view of the participant actor*, any other criterion which will enable the observer to differentiate them, as it were, from the outside?

Durkheim does offer such a criterion. A social fact, he tells us, is 'every way of acting which is general throughout a given society, while at the same time existing in its own right independent of its individual manifestations.'

Now the one class of facts which fits both Durkheim's definition is that of laws, for these are clearly both external to the individual in the subjective sense, and also exist in their own right independently of the uniformities of behaviour to which they give rise. Thus one would expect Durkheim to place a high importance on legal codes as a source of data, and this is what he does, especially in *The Division of Labour*.

But two points should be made, lest we rush to the conclusion that here we have an adequate cut-and-dried demarcation of

[1] Durkheim, *The Rules of Sociological Method*, p. 1.

sociological data. The first is that the empirical study of laws is itself a complex methodological procedure and the second that the range of sociological data is by no means exhausted by the study of laws.

On the first point, it is important to ask what it means to say that laws exist both 'generally throughout a given society' and 'in their own right, independent of their individual manifestations'. What exists is, on the one hand, a uniformity of behaviour amongst a majority of a population and, on the other, a piece of paper with words on it. What connection is there between these two, and what right have we to assume either that given the piece of paper there will be a uniformity of behaviour or vice versa? The answer, of course, might be given that we have discovered empirically that the 'piece of paper' denotes a tendency on the part of other people to use sanctions against potential non-conformists. Thus it was to be expected that at one phase of his development Durkheim would focus his attention on these sanctions as the main type of social fact.

But another answer is that we are mistaken in supposing that laws are simple empirical facts. We are too readily impressed by the image of rolls of parchment or stone tablets and hence tend to think of law as a quasi-material object. But the essence of the law is not in the material through which it is published, but in its meaning. Is this meaning something which can be studied empirically apart from the behaviour of the individuals whom it affects?

Surely the truth of the matter is that the 'piece of paper' has an effect on the behaviour of actors, because they recognize that there is a probability that non-conformity with its dictates would mean the application of sanctions against themselves. This recognition might perhaps be thought of as due to conditioning in a Pavlovian sense, but it would be far more in accordance with our own experience to say that, when we recognize the 'piece of paper' as containing 'laws', we are theorizing about it. In other words the acceptance of the piece of paper as containing binding instructions is due to the existence of what we have called 'participants' theories' about their world. Does not Durkheim's resort to legal codes as a source of sociological data therefore mean a resort to 'participant's theories' as a means of explaining uniformities of behaviour? The view taken here is that this is what Durkheim does do.

Moreover, there would be no harm in this, if he were to recognize what he was doing. Participant's theories are a very useful source from which hypotheses might be drawn and theories constructed. Once this were done we would be able to confront observed uniformities of behaviour with theoretical explanations of the form 'These individuals may be thought of as constrained in their conduct by a law requiring conduct C'. The proof of such a proposition would lie in reports either of the application of sanctions to non-conformists or of expressed beliefs on the part of participants that such sanctions would be applied. When we say that the law exists apart from the uniformities of behaviour of the individuals who accept it, this is what we mean. The notion of 'a law' is something which the participants and observers construct to explain economically the correlation between the uniformities of participants behaviour, the independent existence of a piece of paper with writing on, and the application of sanctions or the belief in the likelihood of their application.

These formulations may appear needlessly pedantic, but they do help us to avoid some of the difficulties which Durkheim encounters when he attempts to deal, as he necessarily must with other sorts of data than legal codes. For when he does so he is searching all the time for empirical or quasi-empirical entities equivalent to laws.

No such entities appear to exist in some cases. They do, of course, in what Durkheim calls 'the ways of acting' imposed on us by education. But they do not either in the case of the uniform behaviour of crowds or in the case of the sorts of statistical regularity indicated by the suicide rate, these being two kinds of social phenomena with which Durkheim was much concerned. In the first case he seeks a way out of the problem by pointing some sort of 'social current' or 'group mind'.

Thus he writes:— 'There are other facts without such crystallized form which have the same objectivity and the same ascendancy over the individual. These are 'social currents'. Thus the great movements of enthusiasm, indignation and pity in a crowd do not originate in any one of the particular individual consciousnesses. They come to each one of us from without and carry us away in spite of ourselves.'[1] Here again, of course, Durkheim is deriving his social facts from the subjective

[1] *Ibid.*, p. 4.

45

experience of individuals and the subjective experience here is one of a powerful external force. But this force is not something tangible or observable and both the participants themselves and sociologists have been much more hard put to it to give an account of any independently existing entity here than in the case of the constraint of law. Durkheim amongst others has been accused of accepting the 'group mind' fallacy, because of his own attempts to give an account of this kind. The point to be made, however, is not that the concept of a group mind as such is illegitimate. Provided that its meaning is made clear and statements about it are made in a verifiable form, there is no reason why it should not be introduced as a theoretical model. What is illegitimate is the reification of the concept, which is inevitable if we follow Durkheim's rule that a social fact must be regarded as existing independently of its individual manifestations.

In discussing the problem of the regularities of behaviour indicated by the suicide rate, Durkheim again refers to 'social currents'. But in this case it is strikingly evident that these social currents are not necessarily experienced as such by the participant actors. Hence Durkheim is forced to recognize that some sort of theoretical construction is necessary in order to explain the separate and individual phenomena, as socially determined. As he puts it:—

No doubt this distinction (between the independently existing social facts and their manifestations) does not always manifest itself with equal directness, but its obvious existence in important and numerous cases just cited is sufficient to prove that the social fact is a thing distinct from its individual manifestations. Moreover, even when this dissociation is not immediately apparent it may often be disclosed by certain devices of method. Such dissociation is indispensable if one wishes to separate social facts from their alloys in order to observe them in a state of purity. Currents of opinion, with an intensity varying according to the time and place, impel certain groups either to more marriages, for example, or to more suicides, or to a higher or lower birth rate etc. These currents are plainly social facts. At first sight they seem inseparable from the forms they take in individual cases. But statistics furnish us with the means of isolating them. They are, in fact, represented with considerable exactness by the rates of births, marriages and suicides . . .[1]

---

[1] *Ibid.*, p. 7.

We should say here that the social currents are theoretical variables introduced by the sociologist and that the statistical rates are the means of obtaining verification for propositions referring to these variables. Or to put this in another way the theoretical variables, the social currents, are operationally defined in terms of the collection of particular statistics.

But Durkheim does seem to have groped his way here towards a much more satisfactory demarcation of social facts than his predecessors. He may be wrong in his reification of theoretical entities, but he did realize that these entities whatever their methodological status, were quite distinct from those of any other science. Moreover, being the positivist he was, he was not content to leave their description vague. Recognizing that his social currents are not observable he insists that 'devices of method' must be introduced in order that empirical verification should be made possible.

It is important to notice that the case of the suicide rates is the best example given by Durkheim of the way in which social facts must be studied. In the earlier examples which he gives, his mis-guided quest for some independently existing 'thing' as the subject for sociological study prevents him from seeing the methodological complexity of the sociologist's task. In the case of the social causes of suicide he is forced by the obvious absence of any such 'thing' to carry out the necessary process of theoretical construction and operational definition before he can begin the study of this class of social facts.

THE SCIENCE OF CULTURE AND THE SCIENCE OF SOCIETY

It would seem then that, if we are to follow Durkheim, the typical social facts are laws and customs, the content of educa-tion and currents of opinion. And even if we insist on greater methodological clarity in recognizing that these are not things but theoretical constructs through which we explain uniform-ities of behaviour, we must admit that Durkheim has made a useful analysis of the specifically social determinants of our behaviour. But there are further problems here which require our attention.

Laws and customs, the content of education and currents of opinion may all be readily included in Tylor's classic definition of culture as 'that complex whole which includes knowledge, art, belief, morals, law, custom, and any other capabilities acquired by man as a member of society'.[1] Is sociology then to be defined as the science of culture? If so what is the relation of this definition of the field to the commonly accepted definition of sociology as the science of society?

Durkheim was always preoccupied with the problem of why rules of behaviour should be regarded as binding amongst human beings, and, as Parsons has shown, he eventually found his way to a view of this problem far more thorough-going than any of his predecessors. We shall return to this problem in a later chapter. Here it should be noted that one strand in Durkheim's thought led him continually to the view that there was an entity 'society', which had moral authority over the individual and that it was because the laws, customs and other normative aspects of our social heritage were the rules of society that we accepted them as binding.

But what do we mean by society? Is it indeed an entity which we can discuss without breaking it down into its elements. Radcliffe Brown notes the problem when he writes:—

> At the present moment of history the network of social relations spreads over the whole world, without any absolute solution of continuity anywhere. This gives rise to a difficulty which I do not think sociologists have really faced, the difficulty of defining what is meant by the term 'a society'. They do commonly talk of societies as though they were distinguishable discrete entities, as, for example, when we are told that society is an organism. Is the British Empire a society or merely a collection of societies? Is a Chinese village a society, or is it merely a fragment of the Republic of China?
> If we say that our subject is the study and comparison of human societies we ought to be able to say what are the unit entities with which we are concerned.[2]

There are actually two problems here. One is the problem of where to draw the boundaries and say 'social relations within this area constitute a society'. But the other problem is much more important. It is that of defining societies in operational terms so that we know what to observe in order to verify propositions about any particular society. This would involve the construction of complex theoretical models whose elements

[1] Tylor, *Primitive Culture* (1924), p. 1.
[2] Radcliffe Brown, *Structure and Function in Primitive Society* (1952), p. 193.

had some sort of reference to observable facts. The suggestion to be made here is that the crucial element in such sociological models is that of social relations, and that it is only through an analysis of the term 'social relation' that the link can be established between the theory of social systems on the one hand and the observation of human behaviour on the other. In fact, unless this analysis is made, any discussion of societies is neither understandable in itself, nor applicable to the explanation of human behaviour.

The fact is, however, that a great deal has been written about human societies, without any such analysis of its constituent elements. This has only been possible because of the substitution of analogy for theory, above all because of the substitution of the organic analogy. There is no objection in principle to the use of such an analogy. Indeed there might be much to be said for it in certain circumstances. If we were doing research in a new scientific field and discovered that there were certain factors operative there, for which there were no adequate theoretical model, it might be extremely useful to take over a model which had been successfully used in some other science and investigate whether it could be used to explain the facts observed in the new field. But this is not the way in which the analogy between societies and organisms has been used. Instead of providing operational definitions for the terms used and seeking to verify statements about the operation of the 'organic' elements by reference to social behaviour, the model provided by the analogy has been itself regarded as providing verifications for sociological propositions.

Of course, no one today would employ the analogy in the way in which it was employed by, say, Herbert Spencer. But it is nonetheless worthwhile emphasizing the dangers in theoretical thinking of this kind, because very often the inadequate theory of many modern sociologists drives them back towards unscientific conceptions which involve some of these dangers.

Durkheim himself is not entirely blameless in this respect. True, he never developed the organic analogy at any length in his attempts to explain the workings of societies. But he did fail to develop any alternative theoretical analysis and his recurring references to the function of social institutions suggest that the analogy was not far from his mind. A quite central fact about Durkheim's sociology is that because of his emphasis

49

upon the externality of social facts he could never really begin to analyse the elementary concept of a social relation. If he had done this, 'society' could not have had the somewhat mystical appearance which it always has in his sociology.

But the organic analogy has had an even more pernicious effect in modern anthropology where it has been used by Radcliffe-Brown and others as a means of justifying the methodological approach to sociological problems known as 'functionalism'. Here the organic analogy has the effect not merely of inporting alien concepts into sociology, but actually demands the substitution in sociology of the concept of function for that of cause. This is something to which Durkheim explicitly objected, despite his own use of the concept of function, and it appears prima facie to involve the acceptance of certain metaphysical assumptions which have no place in empirical science. The next chapter will be devoted to a detailed analysis of functionalism to see whether it is ever possible to avoid making these assumptions when employing the functionalist method. Here it is sufficient to point out that, however useful the organic analogy is in explaining the meaning of the term 'function', it does not help us to demarcate the observable facts, which are relevant to the verification of sociological propositions.

The fact is that, although we are so familiar with terms like 'group', 'community' and 'society' because we continually think in terms of them in our own everyday social life, they are actually complex theoretical constructs. We are able to use them in practical life because there is practical agreement on their use. But when we attempt to talk scientifically about society, the theorizing which we have done in the construction of such concepts has to be made explicit. They have to be broken down into their elements and these elements have to be defined operationally.

THE MEANING OF THE TERM 'SOCIAL RELATION'

The elementary unit out of which we construct the concept 'society' is that of a social relation. One finds, in practice, that whenever sociologists attempt to define the term 'society' further, they use some such phrase as 'the network of social relations'. But by what right do we go on to speak about social relations after observing human behaviour? And what particular sorts of observed behaviour entitle us to talk in this way?

The first point to make is that we only speak of a social relation when the behaviour of more than one party is involved. As Parsons puts it a social relation is always 'doubly contingent'. But we do not use the term every time we observe the behaviour of more than one person. It is also implied that there is also some subjective understanding on the part of the participant actors of the significance of each other's behaviour. Radcliffe-Brown tries to explain this by saying:— 'A social relation exists between two or more individual organisms when there is some adjustment of their respective interests, by convergence of interest, or by the limitation of conflicts that might arise from their divergence of interests. I use the term interest here, in the widest possible sense, to refer to all behaviour which we regard as purposive.'[1]

But what is an 'interest' and how may we make verifiable statements about the interests of those whom we observe? Clearly, if we follow Radcliffe-Brown the term is to be used to refer to an actor's purpose, that is to say to his desire to bring about some future state of affairs. This is quite understandable and only the most rigid behaviourist would deny that we can find evidence in the statements and other behaviour of people to justify us in talking about their purposes.

But the mere fact that the behaviour of a number of individuals is purposive, does not necessarily justify our speaking of social relations as existing between them, even if their purposes happen to coincide (i.e. if the state of affairs which A desires is that which B is also seeking to bring about). Such a convergence of interest is only productive of social relations, if there is an awareness on the part of A of what B is trying to do. Thus a social relationship is only said to exist when there is some evidence of A expecting certain behaviour from B, over and above any evidence about A's purposes and B's actual behaviour. Indeed neither A's purposes nor B's behaviour are necessarily of any importance. A social relation between A and B may exist even when A has no ulterior purpose outside of the relation itself and it may be said to exist even if the actual behaviour of B deviates from that which A expects. The key category in the definition of social relations is undoubtedly that of 'expectations' of behaviour. If we can show that these exist, that is to

[1] *Ibid.*, p. 199.

51

say if we can show that any individual whom we observe plans his own action on the assumption that another individual will act in a certain way, we are usually justified in speaking of the existence of a social relation. It is because they sometimes serve to provide such evidence that attitudes studies constitute an important source of sociological data.

However, even evidence as to the expectations which A has of B, by itself, may not always indicate the existence of a social relation. Clearly A may be entirely deceived about B. So obviously we should wish to imply in any definition of a social relation that there was some likelihood that B would fulfil A's expectations. This is what Weber has in mind in his definition:—

> The term 'social relationship' will be used to denote the behaviour of a plurality of actors in so far as, in its meaningful content, the action of each takes account of that of others and is oriented in these terms. The relationship thus consists entirely and exclusively in the existence of a probability that there will be, in some meaningfully understandable sense, a course of social action. For purposes of definition there is no attempt to specify the basis of this probability.[1]

The last sentence is important for there is the case in which other people take no account of the behaviour of an individual, but he, having noticed a uniformity in their behaviour, takes account of theirs. This might be the case in some sorts of economic activity (e.g. in market research). Weber's own words 'the action of each takes account of the other' appears to exclude this case, but it is possible to include it.

In the more usual case however A knows that there is a probability of B behaving in certain ways, not by some sort of blind induction from B's past behaviour, but because he knows that B's behaviour is conditioned by known factors such as his purposes, the rules or norms which he is known to accept and his desire to win A's approval. Thus any proof of the existence of these factors and of A's knowledge of them counts as evidence of the existence of a social relation of a particular kind holding A and B.

Thus the following may be listed as the observable phenomena from which the existence of a social relation and its particular nature between two individuals A and B may be expressed.

[1] Weber, *The Theory of Social and Economic Organization* (1947), p. 118.

1. A's purposes or interests.
2. A's expectations of B's behaviour.
3. B's purposes and A's knowledge of them.
4. The norms which A knows B to accept.
5. B's desire to win and keep A's approval.

Even these factors, it is true, are not simply observable behaviour phenomena, but relatively speaking, if we look for evidence of these kinds we shall come much nearer to being able to demonstrate our statements about social relations than if we simply study human behaviour at random. If we define a social relation in terms of these categories we shall come as near as is possible to having defined it operationally.

In many sociological studies, of course, the fourth category of data, 'the norms which A knows B to accept' are the prime source from which the sociologist makes his deductions. That is why Durkheim and many others have placed the study of law at the centre of their work. But it no longer appears here, as the study of law did when we discussed it earlier in this chapter, merely as a part of a cultural tradition external to the actors in a social situation. It appears as a constitutive part of their interaction and relationship. Moreover, it becomes evident what other sorts of data we may fall back on in those many situations where there are no clearly enunciated rules governing the relationship, and why there are alternative sources of data. So long as the defining characteristic of law was said to be its externality this was not apparent. Here we see that the existence of law is one amongst a number of factors which we may take account of in trying to discover one actor's expectation of another.

THE STUDY OF CO-OPERATION AND CONFLICT

There is one further difficulty which we have to encounter before our analysis of the term 'social relation' is complete. This is that we have to decide whether or not to include within our subject matter those cases in which there is a probability that B's action in our model might not accord with A's expectations or desires. In other words is sociology to confine itself to the study of social co-operation or should it also include the study of social conflict?

The first point to notice is that there are a number of different variables involved and that therefore there are a number of different ways in which an actual process of interaction might depart from the model of a stable social relationship which we have had in mind this far. For instance A's knowledge of B's probable behaviour might be inadequate or his deductions about it from available data might be fallacious. In this case, any plans which he may make on the basis of his beliefs about B would miscarry. In the extreme case in which A was totally misinformed or ignorant we should have the state of affairs which Parsons, using the word in a very special sense, calls 'anomie'.[1]

Or again we might find that while A expects and desires a certain course of action X from B, B does not know this, or knowing it, is prepared to sacrifice A's approval and risk the consequences of violating norms governing the situation, because doing X is incompatible with the attainment of his own ends. In this case A and B might approach a situation of complete conflict.

Unfortunately, it is not possible to resolve the problem of whether or not to include cases of this sort merely by saying that we shall only include the study of perfectly working co-operative relations in our studies, because the perfectly co-operative relation is only a polar theoretical case. All actual cases lie somewhere along the continuum between perfect co-operation and perfect conflict and the continuum between perfect co-operation and perfect anomie. The elaboration of the notion of perfect co-operation is valuable, of course, for the development of its further theoretical implications, in particular for the development of the theory of the perfectly stable social system, but empirical study would appear to require the use of other theoretical models as well.

In one form or another this will appear as a major theme in later chapters of this book, where it will be argued that, in reaction against utilitarianism, some theorists, notably Durkheim and Parsons, have unduly restricted the scope of sociology to the study of forms of perfect co-operation. Here, however, we should notice that it is possible and very much more satisfactory to define sociology as the science of social interaction rather than as the science of social relations. The empirical variables which we should study are, in any case, the same. But the concept of social interaction is the wider concept and includes social situations lying at all points on our two continua.

[1] Parsons, *The Social System*, p. 39.

We may, therefore, summarize our conclusions thus far by saying that:—

1. Sociology is the science which attempts to make verifiable statements about social interaction.
2. The data, which are relevant in the process of verification, and which it is the task of the empirical sociologist to observe as accurately as possible, are those stated above.
3. Since the emergence of co-operation is always contingent upon the behaviour of more than one individual any particular case of social interaction will fall somewhere between perfect co-operation and perfect conflict and somewhere between perfect co-operation and anomie.

THE STUDY OF SOCIAL SYSTEMS

Sociology, however, does not confine itself to the study of separate social relations. It seeks to discover necessary connections between one relationship and another and between relationships and the activities which may have the effect of sustaining them. Thus the case of perfect co-operation is dependent upon a complex of other activities being performed. There must be processes of education and socialization of the parties. There must be some system of allocation of facilities and privileges as between individual participants and there must be some system of rule enforcement. Once we had established the existence of a social relationship of a particular kind, therefore, we should predict the occurrence of other actions by the participants or third parties and we should study these in order to see whether our predictions were confirmed. Similarly in cases of anomie or conflict we should make certain predictions about the behaviour of the participants and third parties and the study of this behaviour would be included within the scope of our subject.

The great value of the work of abstract theorists like Parsons is that they have gone on from the analysis of the perfectly co-operative relationship (what Parsons calls an 'institutionalised relation') to theoretical speculation about the nature of the sustaining activities. Apart from Parsons' work, Malinowski's posthumous essays published under the title *A Scientific Theory of Culture* may be cited as an attempt to do this.[1] Without such

[1] Malinowski, *A Scientific Theory of Culture* (1944).

theoretical speculation we should not know what other human behaviour was relevant as data for the sociologist. What has not been undertaken is any serious attempt, through a critical analysis of the elementary concepts of anomie and conflict, to provide equivalent guidance in anomic and conflict situations.

Even when this has been done, however, the limitations of such work should be recognized. Its significance lies in the guidance it gives us as to the sorts of data we should seek to collect in the study of any situation of social interaction. But actual social research needs less abstract and more specific guidance than this. In any particular research project we should be concerned to discover what sustaining activities were necessary not merely as the precondition of social relations in general, but as the precondition of particular social relations. In practice the necessity of any particular sort of social system depends upon whether or not the particular social relation which it sustains is thought of as necessary. The research worker seeking to decide which data are relevant therefore always faces a problem of choosing his starting point in his analysis of social situations.

The fact is that there is a division of theoretical opinion here with Parsons, Malinowski and the functionalists on one side and a line of writers including Weber, Mannheim and Myrdal on the other.[1] The former are concerned with describing systematically the sustaining activities necessary for the maintenance of social structures in general, the latter with describing those activities necessary for the maintenance of particular social relations. The division between the two sorts of theory will be explored in the following chapters.

For the moment we may add to our conclusions about the scope of the subject matter the following:—

4. Conceptual analysis of the concepts of perfect social co-operation, perfect conflict, and perfect anomie suggests other sustaining activities performed by the participants or third parties which are relevant as sociological data.
5. While it may, in any case, be asserted that some such sustaining activities are necessary for any situation of interaction, particular forms of sustaining activity are

[1] *See* Weber, *The Methodology of the Social Sciences;* Mannheim, *Ideology and Utopia* (1940); Myrdal, *Value in Social Theory* (1958).

necessary, only in so far as the original interaction situation which gave rise to them is necessary. In a social system those activities which sustain one sort of interaction situation may well disrupt other social situations. This will always occur except in the limiting case of a perfectly integrated social system. One should therefore expect to discover conflict and anomie on the social system level of analysis as much as one does on the level of the analysis of particular interaction situations.

We have now completed our survey of the sorts of data which are relevant for the sociologist. Given these data, we will go on to put forward verifiable proportions about situations of social interaction and about social systems. It may help to clarify the situation further by saying something of the relation between sociology and allied disciplines.

In the first place it would appear that there is a very close relationship between sociology as the study of social interaction and social systems, pyschology as the study of personality systems, and the scientific study of culture in all its aspects. Human behaviour is the data with which both pyschology and sociology begin, but whereas the former is concerned with the relation between the different actions of the same individual, sociology is concerned with interaction, that is with the relationship between the actions of one individual and another. Both sociology and the scientific study of culture, on the other hand are concerned with the study of norms, but whereas the student of culture is primarily concerned with the relations between one set of norms and another, the sociologist is interested in the role played by these norms in the process of interaction.

There is, however, a very close relationship between these three disciplines and it is hardly possible to imagine any significant sociological research being undertaken which did not raise problems in the other two fields. This is why the work of Parsons, Shils and others[1] in attempting to elaborate something of a common conceptual system for the sciences of human action has been particularly fruitful.

The relation between sociology and the study of economics and politics is of a different order entirely. The latter are studies

[1] Parsons, Shils, *et. al. Towards a General Theory of Action* (1951).

57

concerned with particular aspects of social interaction. As such they must be thought of as parts of sociology itself. It is true that the development of the state which rationalizes the allocation of legitimate power within a nation, and of complex economic systems to allocate scarce goods to alternative uses makes specialized sciences of economics and politics essential for practical purposes. But power and economic allocation are, nonetheless, aspects of all situations of social interaction and a sociology which attempted to leave out these aspects in the attempt to define a completely different field for itself would be of no value to anyone.

Finally another entirely different sort of relation holds between sociology and history and it is one which is exceedingly difficult to define. Broadly speaking the historian is much more empirically minded than the sociologist. He is concerned much more with what actually happened and much less with why it happened. But few historians do in fact find themselves capable of excluding some element of explanation from their work, and all historians assume such explanations every time they use words like 'because'. The point is that some, though not all, of the explanations which are given or assumed, depend upon sociological hypotheses. History can gain considerably from the attempt of sociologists to make these hypotheses explicit and to test them. Equally sociological theory has much to gain from subjecting its hypotheses to the tests of history.

It is obvious then that we cannot conclude from this chapter that there is a clear-cut subject matter for sociology which can be settled by some sort of ostensive definition. The data with which the sociologist must work are the same data as are used by the students of other social sciences. They consist in the last analysis of human behaviour of one sort or another. But sociology's particular task is to devise means of verifying propositions about social interaction. These propositions are of a complex theoretical kind, even though they use the terminology of everyday speech. The man who uses this terminology in everyday speech does not have to prove what he says. The sociologist does. It is for this reason that the most essential step for the clarification of the problems of sociological research is that of methodological clarification, that is to say of distinguishing between problems of observation and problems of theoretical construction. And when this is done it is obvious that the

58

definition of the field of sociology depends above all on the attainment of theoretical clarity.

Thus it would seem that each of our first three chapters points to a common conclusion. In the first chapter we saw that whatever the starting-point of science, whether it worked by way of classification, by searching for general laws or for causes, at some point it depended upon the development of theoretical hypotheses. In the second chapter we saw that much contemporary social research was limited in scope and would be until it had some clear theoretical hypotheses to test. In this chapter we have seen that some sort of theoretical development is necessary even to define the subject matter of sociology. Necessarily then we turn in the following chapters to some of the theoretical problems which appear to be implicit in all sociological research.

IV

THE PROBLEM OF
FUNCTIONALISM

As we have shown in the previous chapters, the empirical study of social facts is a methodologically complex process. We do not observe societies or other social facts directly. All that we can observe is human behaviour, including, of course, linguistic behaviour. But sociology does not claim to be simply the science of human behaviour. It is concerned as Durkheim suggested with a reality exterior to the individual. Hence the question arises of how the gap is to be bridged between the phenomena which we observe and this reality 'exterior' to the individual.

It should be noted that this problem is not peculiar to the sociologist. It might be said that all the physicist observes are 'coloured shapes that move'. Yet he is quite prepared to talk in terms of 'electrons' and 'protons'. That is to say, he employs models even at the lowest level to enable him to draw inferences from one observed fact to another, or to explain the coexistence of observed phenomena. Thus if we are prepared to follow the example of the physicist, there is a way out of the sociologist's dilemma. Moreover, since what the physicist does is similar to what we all do all day and everyday, one wonders why sociologists have been so deeply disturbed by behaviourist scruples.

The important question for the sociologist is not whether he should interpret observed human behaviour in terms of models, but what sort of model he should employ. In the previous chapter, although throughout we insisted upon some sort of

60

operational definition of theoretical concepts, nonetheless concepts were linked in terms of a model of the motivation of a hypothetical actor in the situation. The behaviour observed in these circumstances is given significance in terms of the model. For convenience we might refer to the sort of model used there as a 'subjective' model, because behaviour is understood in terms of its subjective meaning for a hypothetical actor in the situation. Or we may speak, following Parsons, of such studies employing an 'action frame of reference'.

The other sort of model which has been widely employed in sociology is that derived from the analogy between societies and organisms. We must now look in greater detail at the assumptions made when this sort of organic model is used, and at the possibility of statements derived from this model being verified.

THE MODEL OF THE ORGANISM

Now to some extent the organic type of model has fallen into disrepute in sociology, because some of the earlier writers like Herbert Spencer who used it seemed more concerned with preserving the analogy than with using the model as a source of verifiable hypotheses. Thus one finds some historians of sociological theory writing as though the theory of the social organism was a thing of the past, something belonging to the bad old days of the system builders. But this is misleading, for even though there may be an unwillingness to bring the model into the open, it is still used in many sorts of sociological studies, and most especially in social anthropology. Whenever we find the terms 'structure' and 'function' in sociology, there we may be sure the writer has in mind some conception of society as an organism. And this has been made perfectly clear in the paper in which the most famous 'functionalist' anthropologist, Radcliffe Brown, sought to justify the use of the concept of 'function'. Here he makes its dependence upon the organic analogy explicit. It will be useful, therefore, to take a long quotation from Radcliffe Brown's paper as the basis for the discussion in this chapter.

He writes as follows:—

For the further elaboration of the concept (function) it is convenient to use the analogy between social life and organic life. Like

61

all analogies it has to be used with care. An animal organism is an agglomeration of cells and interstitial fluids arranged in relation to one another, not as an aggregate, but as an integrated living whole. For the biochemist it is a completely integrated system of complex molecules. The system of relations by which these units are related is the organic structure. As the terms are here used, the organism is not itself the structure, it is a collection of units arranged in a structure i.e. in a set of relations; the organism has a structure ... As long as it lives the organism preserves a certain continuity of structure, although it does not preserve the unity of its constituent parts. It loses some of its constituent molecules by respiration and alimentary absorption. Over a period the constituent cells do not remain the same. But the structural arrangement of the constituent units does remain similar. The process by which the structural continuity of the organism is maintained is called life. The life process consists of the activities and interaction of the constituent cells of the organism, the cells and the organs into which the cells are united.

As the word function is here being used, the life of the organism is conceived as the functioning of its structure. It is through and by the continuity of the functioning that the continuity of the structure is preserved. If we consider any recurrent part of the life-process such as digestion, respiration, etc. its function is the part it plays in the contribution it makes to, the life of the organism as a whole. As the terms are here being used, a cell or an organism has an activity, and the activity has a function. It is true that we commonly speak of a secretion of gastric fluid as a function of the stomach. As the words are here used, we should say that this is an activity of the stomach, the function of which is to change the proteins of food into a form in which these are distributed by the blood to the tissues. We may note that the function of a recurrent physiological process is a correspondence between it and the needs of the organism.[1]

Applying the analogy Radcliffe Brown continues:—

To turn from organic life to social life, if we examine such a community as an African or Australian tribe, we can recognize the existence of a social structure. Individual human beings, the essential units in this instance, are connected by a definite set of social relations into an integrated whole. The continuity of the social structure, like that of the organic structure is not destroyed by changes in the units. Individuals may leave the society by death or otherwise, others may enter it. The continuity is maintained by the

[1] Radcliffe Brown, *Structure and Function in Primitive Society*, p. 176.

process of social life, which consists of the activities and inter-
actions of individual human beings and of organized groups into
which they are united. The social life of a community is here defined
as the functioning of the social structure. The function of any recurrent activity, such as the punishment of a crime or of a funeral
ceremony, is the part it plays in the social life as a whole and therefore the contribution which it makes to structural continuity.[1]

There are obviously a number of ambiguities in these passages,
but it is nonetheless possible to clarify the main lines of the
analogy, which Radcliffe Brown is seeking to draw diagram-
matically as follows :—

	BIOLOGICAL ORGANISM	SOCIAL ORGANISM
UNITS	Cell	Individual human being
STRUCTURE	Relations between cells	Relations between human beings
ACTIVITIES	Observed behaviour of cells	Observed behaviour of human beings and groups
FUNCTIONS	Activities' role in maintaining the structure or correspondence between the effects of activity and the needs of the structure	Activities' role in maintaining the social structure or correspondence between the effects of the activity and the needs of the social structure

Now there need be no dispute about the categories of 'units'
and 'activities'. Both of them have reference to observable facts.
Theoretical construction begins here with the introduction of
the terms 'structure' and 'function', and in order to decide on
the value of the organic model, what we have to do is to examine
the way in which Radcliffe Brown uses these terms in order to
see (a) whether their theoretical meaning is clear and (b)
whether they are so defined that propositions using the terms
structure and function are capable of being verified.

THE CONCEPT OF STRUCTURE

The term 'structure' is of crucial importance, because according
to Radcliffe Brown's version of functionalism any activity is
regarded as explained when it is shown that it has the effect of

[1] *Ibid.*, p. 178.

maintaining the social structure. But the analogy with the organism seems to suggest that there is more difficulty in observing the structure of a social organism. As Radcliffe Brown himself puts it: 'In an animal organism it is possible to observe the organic structure to some extent independently of its functioning. It is therefore possible to make a morphology which is independent of physiology. But in human society the social structure as a whole can only be observed in its functioning.'[1]

Now we must ask here what exactly Radcliffe Brown means by organic structures being and social structures not being capable of being observed 'independently of their functioning'. Apparently the reason for this is that in the case of animal organisms *the spatial arrangement* of the cells is capable of being observed independently of any question of function. And clearly it is true that the spatial arrangement of human beings has no equivalent significance for the sociologist to that which the spatial arrangement of cells has for the biologist. It can be observed, of course. But the sociologist is not especially interested in it. It is not what he means by the social structure. In fact it must be admitted that, if by organic structure we mean the spatial arrangement of cells, then the term structure is being used in a quite different sense from that in which it is used in sociology, and the apparent clarity of the analogy is shown to be deceptive.

In fact it is only possible to preserve the analogy if we interpret the term structure in biology in a different sense entirely, in a sense more akin to that in which it is used in sociology. We must now see what this sense is and whether it is applicable to biological as well as sociological organisms.

Radcliffe Brown speaks of the social structure being capable of being observed only 'in its functioning'. What does this mean? Strictly speaking Radcliffe Brown has contradicted his own definitions in using this phraseology. For according to his own definition it is activities rather than structures which function. But probably he simply means here that the relations between units can only be deduced from the way in which the activities of one unit affects other units. If this is what is meant by social structure then clearly there is an analogous sense in which one may speak of a biological structure. In both cases the structure may be defined in terms of activities and the effect of these activities on units.

[1] *Ibid.*, p. 180.

But even then there is an important difference between biological and social organisms to notice. This is that the activities in terms of which the biological structure might be defined are the same activities which have the effect of maintaining the structure. In healthy organisms, at least, the activities of the units and organs are almost entirely confined to those which have the effect of maintaining the life of the organism. In the case of social organisms things are quite different. People do things involving the co-operation of other people. But these activities do not necessarily have the effect of maintaining the social structure. The task of maintaining the social structure is fulfilled by a number of secondary activities and these are the strict parallel of the activity of the units of a biological organism.

This has a further important consequence. In the case of biological organisms there is only one sort of explanation of an organic activity possible. We say that is explained when we have shown that it has the effect of maintaining a structure. This would be equally true of the secondary activities in a social system mentioned above. But it would be misleading to suggest that all activities must be explicable in these terms. The primary activities of human beings although they may be socially oriented may not have any role to play in the maintenance of the social structure.

Thus we should conclude that the biological model is only useful in suggesting explanations for some human activities. Individuals engage in various sorts of actions and in the course of doing so, enter into social relations with each other. If it is regarded as necessary that these social relations should be maintained, then the existence of certain other sorts of activities is to be expected. It is in the explanation of these other activities that the biological model might be useful.

THE CONCEPT OF FUNCTION

But we now have to notice that Radcliffe Brown does not say that these activities have the *effect* of maintaining a pattern of social relations or a social structure. He says they have the '*function*' of doing this. What is the justification for using the term 'function' rather than the term 'effect'?

A view sometimes encountered is that the idea of a functional relationship is always appropriate where there is a relation of a part-whole type, and this is the reason sometimes given by sociologists for the use of the concept of function both in sociology and biology. But against this it may be said that there are phenomena which are regarded as systematically inter-connected in terms of a part-whole relationship, where the term function is not used, while in the case of biology, as we shall see later, there are other possible reasons for its use. It would seem to the present writer at least that there is no reason why the relationship between part and whole, as such, should not be described in terms of cause and effect. On the other hand if it is desired to have some special term it might be desirable to avoid using the term function because of its teleological over-tones.

The problem involved in the use of the term function in sociology is precisely that of showing why a term with these teleological overtones is chosen. We are bound to ask whether this term is used because some sort of purposive activity or behaviour is envisaged. It will be worthwhile therefore to consider some ways in which activities may be thought of as having purposes. The following appear to be the most important.

1. The activity may be thought of as having been organized or 'set up' for a particular purpose, this purpose being given, for example in the aims clause of the constitution of associations.
2. The activity may be thought of as being purposive in the sense of directly helping to meet the basic needs of the population.
3. The activity may be thought of as fulfilling the intention of the person who carries it out.
4. The activity may be thought of as maintaining a set of social relations or rights and duties, which is essential for carrying out purposive activities in pursuit of individual and culturally-given ends by a population.
5. It may be thought of as carrying out the purposes of 'Society'.
6. It may be thought of as necessary for the survival of the social structure.

The term can quite clearly be profitably used in the first sense and is so used by people like Royal Commissioners investigating the workings of an institution and making recommendations. If they speak of the function of an activity they mean that the activity has a certain effect and that this effect is in turn a means to the achievement of some overall purpose, which they assume to be desirable. In this context it would also be possible to use the term dysfunction to describe an activity whose effect interfered with the attainment of the overall purpose. There is nothing wrong with the use of teleological language here. Such studies begin by assuming that an institution has a purpose and their object is to judge which activities are conducive to this purpose and which are not.

But studies of this kind are of a practical rather than a purely scientific nature. The sociologist's interest in a situation is of a different kind. He is interested in discovering the determinants of an activity and the significance of the ultimate ends of an institution for him is that their acceptance by the participants might serve to explain their activity. Thus he might use a model of purposive activity for *explanatory purposes*. The explanation takes the form of arguing that given the existence of the end the various activities of the institution are determined.

However, many sociologists and anthropologists have noted that the actual activities of individuals are often not consistent with the declared purposes of the institutions in which they play roles. Thus they have looked for other undeclared and perhaps unconscious purposes with which such activities are consistent. Thus Malinowski distinguishes between the 'charter' and the 'functions' of an institution and Merton between 'manifest' and 'latent functions'.[1]

According to Malinowski the determining factors are simply the biological needs of the population. A particular activity is regarded as explained when it is shown that it satisfies one or other of man's biological needs. In this case again teleological language is justified if we assume that the members of a population wish to survive and wish their fellows to survive.

One might perhaps, in passing, note that this form of explanation is not as simple as Malinowski supposes it is. Biological needs are not all that clear-cut and it is possible for individuals to survive at various levels of need satisfaction. Moreover it is possible for an activity to go on even if it means the actual

[1] *See* Malinowski, *A Scientific Theory of Culture* and Merton, *Social Theory and Social Structure*, Chapter 1.

destruction of a part of the population. So it might well be argued that the activities of the population are determined not by the imperative of satisfying biological needs but by a value system which calls for the satisfaction of their needs at a certain level. In this case, however, we should still be justified in talking of the function of the activities. Their effect (the satisfaction of biological needs at a particular level) is a means to the implementation of the value system.

The third usage of the term function need not concern us. Since no social orientation of action is involved, such explanations belong properly in the field of individual psychology.

In the fourth case, an individual's action is explained as being due to the need to ensure that some other individual's ends are attained. The action is seen as purposive in terms of a model which starts from the ends of the other individual. This however is only the simplest case. The action of C may be thought of as facilitating the action of B which in turn may be thought of as helping A to attain his ends. Thus C's action has a function in terms of A's purposes. So the network of interlocking chains of action may become more and more complex.

When a very high degree of complexity is attained it is sometimes imagined that a particular action has the sole purpose of maintaining the structure of society. But the 'structure of society' is itself something which can be explained. Different societies have different 'structures' because they fulfil different purposes. Thus what passes as necessary for maintaining 'the structure of society' is really only necessary for maintaining a particular set of social relations and that in turn is only necessary given that certain purposes must be attained. If this is true our model of sociological explanations is again cast in terms of purpose and we should not have any qualms about using the term function instead of the term effect.

One further interesting point is whether in a complex system of interaction the purposes to which all activities are directed are the purposes of concrete human beings or not. Clearly there is the case in which the mass of individuals became tools for the achievement of the purposes of the powerful. But it is sometimes also the case that the powerful themselves have no option but to follow certain purposes. Thus when we speak of a society being dominated by the 'profit motive' we do not simply refer to the deliberate pursuit of profits by a small number of individuals, but much more to the fact that the culture pattern demands of the powerful that they should pursue monetary profit. We come close here to talking not of the purpose of individuals, but of the purpose of a system. However, the theoretical model is still seen in terms of the action frame of reference and the element of purposive action justifies the use of teleological language.

The fifth and sixth usages of the term function raise rather different problems. Here we do not encounter the model of a network of purposive individual activity, but rather an entity called society or simply the social structure. In the case of the fifth usage, moreover, this entity is personified and assumed to have purposes of its own. Nadel expresses the view clearly enough when he writes as follows :—

> Consider that all explanations in terms of interdependence lead from one combination of data to other, 'anterior' ones; they present us with an infinitely moving system without beginning or end, even without conscious centres or pivots upon which the interconnected parts revolve. This infinite interaction can be given a beginning and an end only through introducing at some point or points the impetus or goal of an ulterior *purpose*, coming from without the system.[1] Physical science has no warrant to take this step; for it would imply the mystic assumption of an intelligence behind the machine which is the universe, and a Great Engineer who conceived its design. In the study of human society such a step is neither unwarranted nor mystic. Society and culture are made and worked by man. May we not assume that they are made and operate for man? The Great Engineer is merely Man in the abstract, and the Intelligence at the back of all things social, the Human Mind writ large. These are, of course, logical constructions which we, the observers, form out of our data.[1]

Now much of what we have said in our previous chapters would appear at first sight to justify a logical construction of this type if such a logical construction seemed the most economical way of explaining the facts. The question, however, is whether 'the Great Engineer' is really demanded by the facts, or simply by the need to justify a superfluous theoretical concept. If, in the first place, we had simply spoken of effects rather than function would such a theoretical construction be called for at all? It might be argued, of course, that, in the case of a very

[1] Nadel, *The Foundations of Social Anthropology* (1951), p. 368.

complex social system, such as was mentioned above, where the over-riding purpose of the system was capable of being considered apart from any particular group of individuals whose purpose it was, some purely theoretical construction is necessary. But it is to be doubted whether the notion of the Great Engineer is a useful concept of this kind, simply because it is not at all clear.

FUNCTION AND ORGANIC SURVIVAL

Finally, we have to consider the sixth usage of the term function which is Radcliffe Brown's own. This is the usage most closely connected with the concept of the organism. The implication here is that there is some sort of parallel with biology, where the use of a purposive term is justified because certain bodily processes are known to be essential to survival and survival may be thought of as the overriding purpose of the organism. The question is, however, whether it is possible to *demonstrate* in sociology that certain processes are essential for survival in the same way in which it is possible in biology.

Obviously there are important differences between the two cases. In the case of biological organisms it is possible to show that a particular activity has an effect which is conducive to survival, because, if the activity is not performed, the organism dies. Its structure and its units cease to exist. Or at least it becomes ill in ways which are clearly definable. But how far can social organisms be said to die or become ill?

Radcliffe Brown, himself, recognizes that there are important differences. Social organisms, he maintains, do not fall ill or die. They change their structural type. As he puts it:— 'while an organism that is attacked by a virulent disease will react thereto and, if its reaction fails, will die, a society that is thrown into a condition of functional disunity or unconsistency will not die but will struggle towards some sort of eunomia, some level of social health, and may, in the course of this change its structural type.'[1]

Now what is the significance of this for the use of the term 'function'? In biology the justification for its use was that an activity could not merely be demonstrated to have a certain effects, but that, if it were not performed, certain other facts of

[1] Radcliffe Brown, *Op. cit.*, p. 183.

a dramatic kind could be demonstrated, viz. death, disintegration and ill-health. The problem is 'can the fact of a change of structural type be demonstrated as clearly as the facts of death and ill-health?' If they cannot, it would be difficult to argue that the effects of an activity were of 'vital' importance for the social organism.

The difficulty here is that social organisms are always changing and that the differences between normal change and a change of structural type is apparently only a matter of degree. Hence the sociologist would have to make a relatively arbitrary decision as to when a change of structural type had occurred and when the activity whose significance was in question could be said to be fulfilling a vital function.

There are, however, a few cases in which a rough demonstration of this sort might be possible. The first of these is the case of a primitive community which has enjoyed a long period of social stability and in which, when it has come into contact with Western civilization, certain activities of a traditional sort have been displaced, and their displacement has led to a period of extensive instability and rapid change in this sort and other sorts of activity. One might have doubts in some cases about the assumption that the particular society was in fact stable in the precontact period. (Recent research amongst the peoples of Southern Africa for example shows how dubious such an assumption is.) But nonetheless one might agree that, relatively speaking, we had sufficient evidence here of stability followed by instability to justify our speaking of the displaced activities as having had a function in promoting the survival of the earlier structural type.

Again we might obtain similar evidence in the comparative study of civilized communities. Suppose, for example, we found two communities with a similar pattern of life, and in one of these some new activity appeared displacing an older form. It might be the intrusion of some new industry, or it might be the acceptance of a new religion by the people. Whatever it was, if its introduction was followed by extensive instability in the pattern of activities, while in the unaffected community people went stably on their accustomed ways, we should be able to speak of the function of those activities which were displaced in one community and which continued in the other.

It must be noted however that it is essential to have evidence

71   F

of stability followed by instability in the pattern of social activities, before we can speak in this way. Too often anthropologists have regarded change as necessarily dysfunctional. When they are asked to show why they regard it in this way, they contrast the new social pattern with the old, claiming that the old represents the healthy social organism. But this standard of health has to be defined by contrast with unhealthy or unstable states, so that, in effect, stability is defined in terms of instability and instability in terms of stability.

Even more serious a lapse is the attribution of functions to activities in a society studied at a single moment of time. If it is suggested that the term function is justifiable because what is claimed is that if the activity alleged to have a function were not performed, the structure or a part of it would collapse, or be temporarily dislocated and then change its type, then it must not be used, except perhaps hypothetically, until there is evidence as to what does in fact happen when it is not performed. Yet it would seem to be almost the normal practice of anthropologists to use the term function as loosely as this.

It seems likely that when this is done, anthropologists are in fact falling back on an entirely different usage of the term function. Implicitly they are using it in the fourth of the senses listed above, where the effect of a particular activity is seen as conducive to the maintenance of a system of social relations, which is in turn conducive to the attainment of certain ulterior ends. There is nothing wrong with this sort of explanation, provided that there is evidence of such ulterior ends playing a determining role in the society. The danger is that if the nature of the theoretical model which is unconciously being used is not made explicit, the anthropologist is likely to interpret as 'functional' those activities which fit into his own scheme of goals and values, and what is more, represent them as essential to the survival of the society. It cannot be too strongly pointed out that explanations of social activities as performing functions in this sense carry no implication that without these activities the society would not survive. All that they imply is that without them certain goals would not be achieved.

In certain instances, then, there is a tendency for sociologists, who start by giving functional explanations in the sense appropriate to the organic theory, to fall back on explanations of a different sort. This latter sort of explanations in no way depends upon the organic model. It depends upon a theory of social interaction.

Merton's famous critique and defence of the functionalist method in his essay 'Manifest and Latent Functions' does not, unfortunately, help to clarify these problems. He insists throughout his essay that, although motivations must be included in the data collected for purposes of functional analysis, nonetheless function has nothing to do with motivation. 'Motive and function', he tells us 'vary independently.' He also holds that some concept of the needs of the social system is vital to sociological analysis. Yet he can do no more than note as a problem the difficulty of establishing such needs objectively, and the actual cases which he quotes of 'latent functions' appear to refer quite definitely not to the needs of the system but to the purpose of groups of individuals.

Thus in his 'Paradigm for Functional Analysis' he has this to say about the category of needs:—

> Embedded in every functional analysis is some conception tacit or expressed, of the functional requirements of the system under observation. As noted elsewhere this remains one of the cloudiest and empirically most debatable concepts in functional theory. As utilized by sociologists, the concept of functional requirement tends to be tautological or ex post facto; it tends to be confined to the conditions of survival of a given system; it tends, as in Malinowski, to include biological as well as social needs.
> This involves the difficult problem of establishing types of functional requirements (universal vs. specific; procedures for validating the assumption of their requirements; etc.)[1]

Yet despite this he is quite prepared to define the term 'functions' as including 'those observed consequences which make for the adaptation or adjustment of a given system.' But what is 'adaptation' supposed to mean? Apparently adaptation to a set of needs of the system which cannot be objectively determined.

Thus, when he comes to draw his distinction between manifest and latent functions, Merton has to either redefine latent functions as meaning 'unintended consequence', a term which

[1] Merton, *Op. cit.*, p. 52.

raises no difficulties about adaption to needs, or to suggest some degree of adaptiveness about the consequences which has reference to the motives and purposes of individuals. For example as instances of the sociologist's investigation of 'latent functions' Merton gives the following:—'the consequences of the new wage plan, for, say, the trade union in which the workers are organized or the consequences of a propaganda programme, not only for increasing its avowed purposes of stirring up patriotic fervour, but also for making large numbers of people reluctant to speak their minds when they differ with official policies'.[1]

Here we have (a) a reference to 'consequences' (b) seen as functional or dysfunctional from the point of view of the motives of certain groups such as trade unionists, people wanting to speak their minds and people not wanting other people to speak their minds.

What we find, in fact, is that, despite the verbal ambiguity which enables it to give the appearance of solving some of the traditional problems of functionalism, Merton's essay does not show how 'consequences' can be thought of as 'adaptive' without making reference to some concept of motive and purposive action. He thinks that he has found a justification for functionalism because he has seen the very real difference between explaining an action in terms of its intention and explaining it in terms of another purposive model which does not refer to the intentions of the actor carrying out the action to be explained. But this other purposive model need by no means be one which requires the establishment of the needs of a social system. It might simply be that implied in our fourth usage, a model to which Merton gives all too little attention. In fact our consideration of the views of functionalist theorists leads inevitably to the view that for greater precision in the formulation of sociological hypotheses a far more detailed model analysing the network of social interaction in terms of the motives of hypothetical actors is absolutely essential. We shall return to a consideration of such a model in the following chapter.

THE CLAIMS AND THE WEAKNESSES OF FUNCTIONALISM

Before we leave the discussion of functionalist theory, however,

[1] *Ibid.*, p. 66.

it is worth noticing that there are certain features of the functionalist approach which account for its widespread appeal. It does serve to meet certain important problems which are peculiar to sociology and it is worthwhile listing these, so that when we do turn to the elaboration of another model, we shall be able to ask whether it is able more adequately to deal with these problems.

The claims of functionalism appear to be as follows:—

1. It has emphasised the importance of the social as distinct from the individual determinants of human behaviour.
2. It has drawn an important distinction between explanation in terms of the motives of individuals and explanations in terms of the requirements of social systems.
3. It has excluded speculation about human motives and has thus appeared to meet the behaviourist type of criticism of sociology.
4. It has sought to substitute objectively determinable factors (e.g. the needs of the social structure) for purely subjective ones as the determinants of social systems, thus attempting to exclude all value judgements from sociology.
5. It has done justice to the fact that social activities do not merely have immediate and isolated consequences but also systematic long-term ones.

These are extremely important claims and it is because it makes them that functionalism has to be taken seriously as a contribution to sociological theory. Nonetheless it may be asked whether the degree to which functionalism meets the requirements of sociological theory, which it itself sets out, is not more apparent than real.

The consideration which we have put forward in this chapter, for instance, would lead us to ask some of the following questions:—

1. Is not the effect of functionalism's attempt to demarcate social and individual determinants of human behaviour in a hard-and-fast way merely to produce an obscure definition of the social?
2. Does the true distinction between the social and individual determinants of behaviour not lie in the fact that the former is the product of social interaction and is this concept not

closely akin to, though much more complex than, the concepts in terms of which individual action is explained?

3. Does not the attempt to exclude all discussion of purpose from sociological analysis result in the exclusion of an illuminating and legitimate source of data?

4. Are value judgements really excluded by relating activities to the needs of the system or are they merely concealed in the obscure definition of these needs?

5. Does not the validity of the whole approach rest upon the applicability of the notions of 'survival value' to human activities and is this notion really applicable?

Serious consideration of these questions must serve to throw doubt on the functionalist approach. The 'needs of the system' cannot be so decisively demonstrated as functionalism supposes, because of the difficulty of demonstrating that any activity is vital for the system's survival. Hence what often passes for such a demonstration is the explanation of an activity in terms of the contribution which it makes to the attainment of certain ends, the necessity of which the functionalist takes for granted. Similarly functionalism only appears to exclude reference to subjective motives. As we saw in the examples of 'latent functions' given by Merton above, in practice the functionalist does relate institutions and activities to the aims of individuals and groups. It would be much better therefore to acknowledge this, and to seek to show clearly through empirical proofs what aims, ends or purposes are held by the participants in the situation.

On all these points then, functionalism would appear to be making false claims. It appears valid only when we require only the roughest of proofs. This may be the case when we are witnessing a rapid period of social change such as occurs in the social contact situation or when we are all agreed that certain 'needs of the system' must be satisfied. But as soon as we demand any exact definition of the categories of 'survival value' or the 'needs of the system' we find that they cannot be given.

One point raised by functionalism, however, does withstand criticism. This is the fifth of those mentioned above, and the point behind Merton's distinction between manifest and latent functions. There is a distinction between the immediate and isolated and the long-term and systematic consequences of an activity. If, therefore, we seek to replace functionalism with a model based upon the notion of interaction, we should see to it that this model is capable of emphasising the same distinction.

It is, however, precisely to the notions of action and interaction that we now wish to draw attention. They are notions which have been regarded with suspicion as not being completely scientific. Yet they do appear to provide illuminating explanations of a kind which functionalism cannot do. Can they then be used in a scientific way? Our problem is not unlike that of Marx in the 'Theses on Feuerbach', where he wrote:—

'The chief defect of all hitherto existing materialism . . . is that the thing, reality, sensuousness, is conceived only in the form of the object of contemplation, but not as human sensuous activity, practice, not subjectively. Hence it happened that the active side, in contradiction to materialism, was developed by idealism, but only abstractly, since of course idealism does not know sensuous activity as such. Feuerbach wants sensuous objects, really differentiated from the thought objects, but he does not conceive human activity itself as objective activity.'[1]

Functionalism, like the materialism which Marx was attacking, tries to exclude subjectively formulated models of action. On the other hand, too often, those who do consider society subjectively, adopt a merely intuitive approach and fail to demonstrate their explanations empirically. Can we not include the subjectively formulated notion of action in our sociological theory and yet demonstrate what we say about action and interaction objectively and empirically? This must be our aim in the ensuing chapters. We need not, by any means, accept the metaphysical implications of Marx' first thesis in doing so, but Marx has achieved an important insight here, and we shall have occasion to return to it when we develop the notion of systems of interaction to take account of social change.

[1] Marx, 'Theses on Feuerbach' in Marx and Engels. *On Religion* (1955), p. 69.

V

THE ACTION FRAME OF
REFERENCE

THE CONCEPT OF ACTION

ANY attempt to understand the meaning of the term
social relation' leads us inevitably to an analysis of the
terms 'interaction' and 'action'. 'Action' is the simplest
theoretical term of all in sociology, and we shall now proceed
to analyse it before going on to show how the more complex
theoretical constructs of sociology may be built up from it.

According to Max Weber, in whose analysis of the fundamental concepts of sociology the notion of 'action' plays a
central part, the defining feature of action is its 'meaningfulness'.
Thus in his famous definition he writes, 'in action is included all
human behaviour insofar as the actor attaches a subjective
meaning to it'.[1]

Two features may be noted about this definition. Firstly, it
starts with a frankly subjective approach to sociological theory.
In this respect the work of Weber, like that of Pareto, is sharply
differentiated from that of Durkheim. But the significance of
this should not be misunderstood. It does not mean that Weber
accepts the intuitive method of 'sympathetic introspection' as
the basis of his sociology. What he is suggesting is that the
theoretical constructs of sociology should be built up from the
basic model of the motivation of a 'hypothetical actor'. The
'hypothetical actor' is a theoretical construction and statements
about his motivations have empirical implications so that it is
possible to verify them 'objectively'. The mistake which is too

[1] Weber, *The Theory of Social and Economic Organization*, p. 110.

78

often made is to suppose that the subjective formulation of theoretical concepts of sociology involves the abandonment of the ordinary canons of scientific proof. Explanations of behaviour in terms of action necessarily involves a subjective formulation of theoretical concepts. But there is no reason why this should be any less scientific than explanation in terms of any other sort of theoretical concepts.

The second feature concerns the meaning of Weber's term 'meaning'. This term was one which had played a large part in the great debate about historiography and the methodology of the Social Sciences in Germany in the period immediately before Weber, and it has many overtones even in Weber's work which derive from this tradition. Nevertheless the sense in which Weber primarily used the term was that which refers any particular behaviour to the purpose or aim of the 'hypothetical actor'. Weber does not confine himself to this case, but he uses the rational type of action (i.e. the case in which behaviour can be understood simply as a means to an end) as a starting point, so that other types can be understood in terms of their deviation from the rational pattern. We may find it useful to proceed in the same way.

We saw in a previous chapter that the concepts of social relation and social interaction were not simple concepts, but that they rested upon a number of variable elements. From these we were able to deduce the three possibilities which we called perfect co-operation, conflict and anomie. But each of these concepts pre-supposed that the action of the various participants in the interaction process was of the rational type. We must now take our analysis to a still deeper and more complex level by an analysis of the rational type of action itself. Here it will emerge that the concept of rational action itself is only one possibility and one which makes important assumptions about the situation of the actor which may not always be fulfilled.

The following assumptions are made when we explain any observed behaviour as following from the rational motivation of a hypothetical actor:—

1. It must be assumed that the end in terms of which the behaviour is explained itself presents no problems. We assume therefore that human beings are capable of formulating any ends which they choose and that we are able clearly to understand those ends.

79

2. It is assumed that given the end there are certain sorts of behaviour which may be understood as necessary means for the attainment of these ends.
3. We assume that the hypothetical actor has the sort of complete knowledge of the situation which a scientist might have attained.
4. We assume that having this knowledge of the means and ends in the situation the actor employs the sort of logical reasoning which an applied scientist might use in carrying out his action.

RATIONAL AND NON-RATIONAL TYPES OF ACTION

But as soon as we set out these assumptions we see that actual human behaviour is often governed by other sorts of motivation. Human ends may not be unlimited. Certain ends may not be sought because they are in some sense taboo. Secondly they may be so hazy that no clear consequences in terms of behaviour could necessarily be thought of as following for the actor. Thirdly there might be cases in which the end was clearly enough defined, but since it was a non-empirical one (e.g. Salvation) nothing appeared to follow as a necessary means. Fourthly it might be the case that the actor's knowledge of the situation was imperfect and that though his action might have been rational had his picture of the world been correct, it appears irrational in the light of the scientist's view of the situation. And finally it might be that, although the actor is well aware of the facts of the situation, he plans his own action in terms of a logic quite different from that of empirical science.

Thus we are often faced in the human sciences with behaviour which defies description in terms of a rational pattern of motivation. This is particularly true of behaviour of a religious or magical kind in all societies and amongst primitive people where such behaviour plays a larger part than it does in modern secular societies. We find that when we are seeking to explain this behaviour, very few of the assumptions of rationality appear to hold. Ends which come naturally to mind as conceivable starting points for explanation are irrelevant because such ends are tabooed by the society. The ends which men do seek are unclear to us and when we do understand them no scientific demonstration of the relation between means and ends is available to us to apply to the explanation. The only way in which we can explain behaviour as being related to ends is through the apparently arbitrary ritual rules of the society in which they find themselves (e.g. in the case of meteorological phenomena, or in the case of the relation between copulation and conception, in both of which cases primitive people have been reported as being ignorant of elementary scientific facts). Or finally they may be well aware of the facts of the situation, as primitive people often are of the facts relevant to agriculture, yet may carry out practices which are not based upon this knowledge or upon ordinary logic at all.

Anthropologists divide in their treatment of such behaviour. Malinowski, for instance, was notable for his insistence on the fact that there was a strong element of reason in the behaviour of primitive people. This was the complement of his insistence on the difference between 'charter' and function. For Malinowski goes beyond insisting that the explanation of behaviour is to be found elsewhere than in the declared intentions of the individual observed. He also wants to explain to us that the savage is not the fool we take him for and that on a deeper level his action can be made to appear profoundly *rational.*

This position of Malinowski's derives very largely from the polemical orientation of his writing. He wants to provide some sort of counterweight to the rather exotic accounts of strange practices in faraway places. And above all he wants to include all human behaviour within a basically utilitarian frame of reference. An adequate account of social behaviour, however, cannot be given in the radical utilitarian terms which Malinowski suggests. There is a great deal which must be taken very seriously in the writings of anthropologists like Levy-Bruhl and Fraser, which Malinowski brushes aside too lightly.[1] True, they may have gone too far in suggesting that the primitive world was governed by a pre-logical mentality which necessarily gave way with the advancement of science. But on the other hand there are aspects of behaviour both in primitive and in relatively civilised societies which defy explanation in utilitarian terms. Frankfurter's essay on 'The Logic of Mythopoeic Thought' may be cited as an illuminating attempt to find another and more satisfactory basis for the explanation of this behaviour.[2]

[1] *See* Levy-Bruhl, *How Natives Think* (1926), and Fraser, *The Golden Bough* (1922). [2]Frankfort *et al., Before Philosophy* (1949), Chapter 1.

The sort of social world which does rely upon purely rational forms of action has been emphasised by many of the great sociologists including Tonnies, Durkheim, Weber and Pareto. But each of these writers saw the rationalistic world as emerging slowly and relatively imperfectly from a background of traditional order unamenable to utilitarian explanation. Thus Tonnies sketched the outlines of Gemeinschaft,[1] Durkheim discussed mechanical solidarity[2] and Weber made the traditional order and primitive religion the starting point for his great analysis of the emergence of modern ideologies and social systems.[3]

Pareto's analysis is particularly interesting because he comes to it from the study of economics, which is precisely the study of the intersection of rational patterns of action by a plurality of actors.[4] His analysis of social systems is essentially an analysis of the residual elements which are left over when the economist's analysis has been, as it were, abstracted out. His emphasis is on the non-logical theories in terms of which action of a non-logical sort may be explained. He probably oversimplified the picture by trying to extend his concept of residues (i.e. the non-logical theories) to account for all possible deviations from the rational case, and would have done well to have introduced other categories, but he does have the merit of having restored to an important place in sociological theory the notion of action of a non-rational type.

Weber's two categories of traditional and affectual action are unfortunately scarcely developed in his work. They remain merely the starting point with which rationality of motivation is contrasted, but he is particularly clear in his analysis of the complexity of economic action and shows that there is more to this than merely a rational decision to use the technically most efficient means for the attainment of ends. The normal mode of economic action is what Weber calls Zweckrationalitat which is defined as action involving the rational weighing of alternative courses of conduct in terms of their utility to the actor. This is a complex category and quite distinct from that Weber calls Wertrationalitat.[5] The latter refers to the single minded pursuit

---

[1] Tonnies, *Community and Association* (1955).
[2] Durkheim, *The Division of Labour in Society.*
[3] *See* Parsons, *The Structure of Social Action* (1949), pp. 563–578.
[4] Pareto, *The Mind and Society* (1935).
[5] For Weber's discussion of the types of action *see The Theory of Social and Economic Organization*, Chapter 1.

of an absolute value. This is a concept which must occur at two levels in Sociology. It must be used to explain behaviour in cases where questions of utility or questions of which end is to be pursued have been decided. In this case it refers to the technically most efficient form of action. Or it may be used as Weber uses it to refer to ultimate goals in relation to which the ends which are weighed in the case of economic action appear only as means.

The distinction which we have to make in building our theory of social systems is not that between economic and other forms of action, but between rational action, in the sense of using the technically most efficient means and the various non-rational types. If we can begin by giving a simple account of the basic types of action, rational and non-rational, we can go to an analysis of the organization of such unit actions into systems in two ways. On the one hand, we should be concerned with the chains of action of particular individuals, in which what is an end from the point of view of the unit act, appears as a means in the longer chain. And on the other, we should consider the relation of unit acts by one individual to unit acts by another i.e. to the more complex concept of interaction. It is at this level which concepts like Weber's notion of Zweckrationalitat become important.

At the elementary level of the explanation of behaviour in terms of unit acts, however, we must conclude that there is not merely one basic type of action, but a variety of different types. In the first place there are the purely rational types in which the actor has a clear conception of his ends, a scientist's knowledge of what the elements of the situation are and of how these elements must be altered in order to produce as an effect the state of affairs which is desired as an end. A number of variations from this type are also possible. The actor may have an unclear conception of the end or he may place it in relation to a number of other ends, being prepared to rest content with only a partial attainment of his aim. He may through ignorance or through misinformation have a picture of the elements of the situation and of what is required to attain his end different from the objective picture obtained by the empirical scientist. Finally the actual course of behaviour on which he embarks may be inappropriate because of the defective logic of his plan of action. All these cases do occur and may be thought of as basically related to a logical scheme of action.

Distinct from these, however, are actions of a non-rational type. They may be called non-rational because they are not essentially departures from a rational norm. In these cases we have non-empirical ends pursued by the actor and what we shall call 'ritual rules'. These 'ritual rules' occupy the same place in non-rational schemes of action as do the technical rules which govern rational action. It does not appear possible at the moment to define precisely the logic of these 'ritual rules'. They appear to be relatively arbitrary and most attempts to define them have attained only a negative definition. One interesting attempt in the history of sociology to reach a more complete understanding of them is that of Durkheim in his *Elementary Forms of Religious Life*. The surprising feature of this book is that after talking about religious practices and beliefs, Durkheim feels it necessary to expound a full-scale theory of knowledge. In this theory of knowledge he goes beyond giving an account of the significance of the ritual rules which operate in non-rational action, to suggest that the basic categories of scientific thought, themselves, (e.g. space, time and causation) are derived from social experience. Whether or not Durkheim was correct in this, he may, by having made a radical over-statement of the case, have directed our attention in a profitable direction. In suggesting that the norms and logic of rational and non-rational conduct alike derive from social experience, he makes the latter appear far less arbitrary. And by posing the problem as a problem in the theory of knowledge he shows that he is well aware of the role of logical norms in the structure of action.

At all events we have to note at this point that there are unit acts which must be taken into account on our model of a social system, which are governed by logical norms different from those applied in technically rational action. It is a predominance of actions of this sort which serves to characterise Durkheim's society based on mechanical solidarity, Tonnies' 'gemeinschaft' and Weber's 'traditional society'. Is there any other form of unit act which is not included in one or other of the two types we have mentioned?

Possibly there is a third category. Weber, it will be remembered included not merely two types of rational action and traditional action, but a third type which he called 'affektuel'. It would seem useful to retain such a category at least provisionally, for there are actions which it is hard to include in a theoretical scheme of means and ends, without distortion. There are the actions which may be thought of as giving expression to emotional states rather than as being in any sense directed to the attainment of a purpose. It is true of course that the form of expression might be thought of as a means and the emotional release regarded as an end. And it may be that, if this is so, the relationship between means and ends is to be explained in the same way as in the non-rational type of action mentioned above. But until we understand more about 'ritual rules' and symbolic relations, it might be well to include this as a third category.

SOCIOLOGICAL EXPLANATIONS IN TERMS OF ACTION

So we come to the conclusion that the interpretation of human behaviour in the action frame of reference requires the development of at least three major theoretical types of motivation. But so far we have only been concerned with individual action, rather than with the sociologist's main concern which is inter-action. We must now proceed with the process of theoretical construction in a sociological direction.

The first point to notice is that the action of one individual may be integrated with that of another through the cultural patterning of the elements. Precisely because the elements of motivation and action are variable, and because the individual must choose between them, the conduct of any individual may be thought of as flexible and capable of being directed along common lines by learned culture patterns.

In the first place, whether action is rational or non-rational, the ends which the individual seeks may be set for him by his cultural conditioning. Secondly, the picture of the world which he has may be the same as that of his fellows, because the process of getting to know the world is governed by norms which come to him as part of the culture pattern. In this respect our own culture places the major emphasis on the norms of empirical science. But even today other norms of a philosophic, ideological and religious kind are operative here. Similarly one would expect a variety of different culturally patterned norms to operate in the logic of the act itself. It is at this point that we sought to differentiate the rational and non-rational types of unit act. And finally in the case of emotionally governed action, there is the problem of the appropriate symbol for the expression of emotion.

Private symbolism may play a small part here, but the fact is that, by and large, we express our joy, our anger, or our grief through symbols which we learn as being appropriate from our culture.

The sort of motivation of action which we have mentioned thus far, however, is insufficient to sustain a system of inter-action. It is true that if the ends of action are set by the culture pattern it is very likely that the actions of individuals will be integrated and complementary. But this may not be so, and in effect all that we have said so far is that the existence of culture patterns ensures that individuals will act in terms of a common social idiom. This will have many advantages from the point of view of the building of social systems. Above all it will ensure that the individuals concerned will be able to understand one another's action. But this does not mean that their actions will necessarily be integrated with one another.

Social action, as distinct from action in general, begins according to Weber when 'the action of one individual takes account of the action of others and is thereby oriented in its course'. Thus, given the motivation of the individual, and given that he is able to interpret the behaviour of other individuals we may sometimes be able to interpret his action as social action in the Weberian sense.

In a previous chapter we laid emphasis upon one particular type of social interaction, namely that in which the action of the parties to the interaction was purposive and rational. This is one important case. Perhaps it is the most important. But in principle any of the sorts of motivation which we have mentioned may give rise to social interaction, whether it is of the rational, non-rational or of the expressive emotional type. In the first case A takes account of the behaviour of B as a means or as a condition in this attempt to attain his ends. Equally in the second case what B does may be relevant to the carrying out of A's action in accordance with ritual rules. And in the third case B's behaviour may be assigned some role in A's attempt to give symbolic expression to his feelings.

But a further dimension is added to sociological analysis by the fact that B's behaviour may be regarded not merely as a means or as a condition in A's action, but as an end in itself. Thus there are basically two sorts of social relation, namely the instrumental kind in which B's behaviour is regarded as a means to some ulterior end on the part of A, and the non-instrumental kind in which the end of A's action is to produce certain behaviour from B which he desires for itself.

In any case, if we start by understanding A's motivation in terms of ends, means, conditions, scientific and ritual rules or symbolic expressions we arrive at the conclusion that some of these elements may involve the behaviour of other parties and that the action is then 'social' action. The next point to notice is that the 'social' element in the action may not stop at taking account of the behaviour of B, but that either A may have to take account of the behaviour of many other parties, or that his reading of B's action may be that *it* is socially-oriented, by virtue of taking account of the behaviour of C D E and so on. Thus starting from A's motivation we may go on to build up systems of almost infinite complexity.

At this point, of course, we pass over from psychological to sociological analysis. But this does not mean that the motivation of the hypothetical actor A, from which we started, drops out entirely from our analysis. Weber was very insistent on this point. For him the analysis of social systems always meant analysis in terms of the motivation of a hypothetical individual. He rejected the organic approach or any attempt to treat social systems as wholes apart from the motivation of individuals, except as a means of gaining a preliminary orientation to the field. Thus there is a sharp differentiation of the Weberian type of theory from the functionalist approach in the previous chapter. For Weber, the only possible meaning which could be given to the term function (in fact it is not a term for which he found any use) is the role of a particular action in the plan of action of a hypothetical individual in terms of whose motivation the whole social system was analysed. This tradition of social analysis has, regrettably, been a subordinate one in recent sociology, only a few writers such as Mannheim and Myrdal insisting on it in the face of functionalist orthodoxy.

One of the reasons why this sort of approach to sociological explanation has not been acceptable is that many sociologists fear that it assimilates sociological to psychological explanations, since both are given in terms of motivation. But there is in fact all the difference in the world between the two explanations. Sociological explanations do not explain human behaviour in terms of the determining effect of an individual's own motivation on his overt behaviour. They explain it in terms of the existence of an interaction system such that the behaviour of B is determined by the pattern of motivation of A. It is this fact, that the behaviour of one individual is always explained in terms of the motivation of another, which sharply differentiates sociological from psychological explanation.

Of course this does raise the question of starting points for the analysis of social systems. It could be argued that the Weberian method leaves open the possibility of an infinite number of different accounts of social systems varying according to their starting point. Weber himself accepted and Mannheim and Myrdal have both profitably pursued the implications of this approach. On the other hand it might be argued that in any social system which lasts, one particular form of motivation is dominant and that the task of sociological analysis is to discover which this is and to go on to construct a model starting from the dominant form of motivation. But if we do accept this alternative it should not be thought that we are avoiding reference in our explanation to the motivation of Weber's 'hypothetical actor'. It is still that motivation and not some vague category of the 'needs of the social structure' which is the ultimate determinant of any behaviour occurring within the system.

The model which we should have to construct on this basis would include not only the behaviour of B C D E etc. of which A's motivation took account, but also the various control mechanisms which had the effect of ensuring that this behaviour did fulfil A's expectations. But once again it would need to be emphasised that the ultimate explanation of the existence of these control mechanisms lay in the fact that there was a social system based upon A's motivation. Thus sociology would not be concerned with explaining human behaviour in terms of controls and sanctions. It would be concerned with explaining the controls and sanctions in terms of the necessity of certain behaviour to the continued existence of a social system based upon a particular pattern of motivation. The 'external' facts which Durkheim correctly saw as being the sociological determinants of human behaviour lay not in the controls and sanctions, but in the demands which A's plan of action laid upon B. The controls and sanctions were themselves indirectly determined by these demands.

The particular form taken by the expected behaviour of other parties and the controls and sanctions which sustain it may, of course, be expected to vary with the particular form and content of the motivation of the hypothetical actor around which the social system as a whole turns. And because this form and content is so variable it is hardly likely that we shall be able to discover particular forms of controls and sanctions which are necessary, whatever the determining motivations of the system. Parsons by concentrating his attention on the forms of the basic motivation pattern (what he calls 'the pattern-variables of role expectation') has suggested that the number of possible permutations and combinations is limited and hence there is also for him only a limited number of possible types of controls and sanctions.[1] But when the content of motivation is considered (e.g. the variety of human purposes) it is obvious that there must be greater variety, unless these can be shown to be reducible to a limited number of basic determining needs or purposes of individuals. It is noteworthy that for Weber the starting point of analysis for the modern social order was a whole philosophy of life, rich in its historical content, not a formal value pattern like the 'universalist achievement' pattern which Parsons places at the centre of his analysis. It may be that it will eventually be shown that the distinction between form and content in social action and relations is not as absolute as one might imagine and that the rich historic content of the weltanschaungen of different periods will be shown to be reducible to a small number of types. But this has not yet been done and Weber's analysis of the social system of the Reformation appears for the moment to be more revealing in its explanations than Parsons' formal analysis of social systems in terms of their value patterns.

Again it must be emphasized that the particular form of the controls and sanctions in a social system will vary according to whether the basic interaction situations is one of co-operation, conflict or anomie. Parsons is quite explicit about the fact that he is concentrating on the first case and he has done valuable work in developing his analysis to show what are the institutional prerequisites of social interaction of this kind. Similar analyses could be developed of the institutional correlates of a basic situation of anomie or conflict.

---

[1] *See* Parsons, *The Social System*, p. 58.

Even before this is done, however, it is possible for us to make some general observations about the problem areas of interaction for which there is likely to be some institutional provision in any society. We may assume that this will be the case in any social system because the problems involved occur in any situation of action and interaction. In this matter, the analysis presented by Kingsley Davis in his *Human Society* is useful.[1] Davis actually assumes a basic situation of co-operation, but his argument is couched in sufficiently general terms for us to see its relevance whatever the basic situation with which we are dealing.

Davis deals with the problem of the integration of systems of social action on two levels. First he discusses the role of technical and economic norms in bringing system and order into the unit acts performed by a particular individual, and secondly he goes on to discuss the problems involved in the relationship of the unit acts or chains of unit acts of more than one individual. It is this latter analysis which concerns us here and which is particularly important to the elaboration of a formal picture of any social system.

The first problem which Davis raises is that of economic order as between individuals. This arises from the fact that the supply of facilities which figure as means in the action plans of separate individuals is inherently limited. Hence there is necessarily a problem of allocation of these scarce resources to alternative uses and to different individuals. In other words some sort of property system is to be expected in any working social system.

This does not, of course, settle any questions about the necessity of any particular type of property system and it should not be thought that it contributes anything to the great debate about the inevitability of private property which has played a great part in the history of anthropological and sociological research. Nor need we assume that every individual will accept the property system which exists. All we need say is that if there is a dominant pattern of motivation in the social system that pattern of motivation implies that there will be some attempt to provide systematically for the allocation of scarce goods between alternative uses.

[1] Davis, *Human Society* (1955), Chapter 5.

Whether or not the participants in the social system all accept the property system as morally binding on themselves, however, is another matter. They may clearly resort to fraud or force. Davis sees this possibility not merely as one which may occur in some cases but as a normal feature of social systems. Hence he goes on to argue that the property system must be backed by political institutions, that is to say institutions which have the task of allocating, not facilities for social action, but the right to use power to compel other individuals to act in expected ways.

This however only pushes the problem one stage further back. For the notion of a *right* to use power presupposes that there is some agreed conception of rights or 'legitimacy', and this, of course, is the third problem area of social systems to which Davis draws attention. In a stable social system as he sees it, some set of ultimate values is necessary, in terms of which certain actions and the use of power in support of these actions can be shown to be legitimate. To give this more general significance we should say that those who wish to see a certain basic pattern of action facilitated would always propose a set of ultimate values to legitimate the use of power in support of certain actions and a certain system of allocation of resources.

At this point, however, Davis notes an important problem. This is that the ultimate values are not necessarily accepted for their own sake. They are too far removed from the point of giving real satisfaction and rewards for that. Instead of being accepted for their own sake, therefore, they are often bound in with the beliefs of individuals about non-empirical entities and the sorts of actions which are required in relation to these entities. In other words behaviour in conformity with the needs of the interaction system is accepted not because it is thought to be in conformity with the system but because it happens to be in the behaviour which is enjoined by the religious beliefs and the ritual rules of the society. Thus the non-rational unit acts which we discussed at the very base of our model are shown to have a function at its apex.

As Kolb has noted, however, Davis' position on this matter is very tentative.[1] We should probably agree that any interaction system has problems regarding economic allocation, power, and the development of an ultimate value system. Each

[1] In Becker and Boskoff, 'Modern Sociological Theory' (1957).

of these is presupposed by the one before it. But it is less obvious that religious belief and ritual are presupposed by the ultimate value system. It is true that some means must be found of inculcating ultimate value attitudes, but there is no necessary reason why this means should be religious belief and ritual. Moreover religious belief and ritual might have a quite independent role within the system.

In fact the role of religion in social systems is one of the most perplexing problems in sociological theory. Davis, as we have seen, like Durkheim before him, sees religion as being the means whereby ultimate values are underpinned. But, as in the case of Durkheim, we feel bound to ask whether this means that religion is explained in terms of the ultimate values of the social system or vice versa. There is a tendency in the work of Parsons and Davis to take the latter view, though it is not explicit. But there is the alternative view expounded for instance by Marx, when he says 'the secret of the Holy Family must be found in the earthly family'.[1]

This creates a very practical problem in sociological analysis. It is the problem of how to treat the non-rational unit acts at the base of our model. Is it our task to seek to explain these by showing their relation to unit acts of a rational kind through the mediation of the institutions of control or are they to be accepted as separate elements in the system? This must unfortunately still be regarded as an unresolved problem of sociological theory. It is no answer to say that the non-rational *must* be reduced to the rational, since there are still non-rational acts which defy explanation in these terms. It is, of course, the duty of the sociologist to exhibit such relationships and dependencies as can be exhibited. But he cannot declare in advance that it will be possible to do so in all cases. To some extent then it may be necessary to say that some non-rational actions are irreducible.

A MODEL FOR THE ANALYSIS OF INTERACTION SYSTEMS

With this in mind, we may now draw out some conclusions about the sort of model which is involved in explaining human behaviour as the product of social interaction. The object of such a model is to enable us to explain why any particular

[1] Marx, 'Theses on Feuerbach'.

aspect of human behaviour which is thought to have social determinants takes the form which it does. In this, as in all models used in scientific explanation, there must be some particular empirical phenomenon whose existence is not thought of as requiring explanation. All other empirical phenomena coming within the frame of reference of the model are explained by showing their relationship in terms of the model to this key phenomenon.

The starting point of our model is the notion of the unit act. In the simplest case this may be thought of as including a hypothetical actor who has a purpose (i.e. who wishes to bring about some future state of affairs) and manipulates certain means in certain conditions in order to attain that purpose (the conditions are distinguished from the means in that, though they are relevant to the attainment of the purpose, they are beyond the control of the actor). We should say that the behaviour of an observed individual is explained if there were evidence that he desired the state of affairs which occurred as the effect of his behaviour. The justification for our saying this lies in the fact that we accept a theoretical proposition about a hypothetical actor acting purposively.

Not all human behaviour is capable of explanation in terms of such propositions, however, and, hence, other theoretical propositions must be used to explain individual human behaviour. These refer to non-rational and affective action. In these cases we should say that the behaviour was explained if there was evidence that the observed individual desired a particular state of affairs and also accepted certain ritual rules as to the way in which that state of affairs should be attained; or if there was evidence of the individual being in a particular emotional state and accepting certain forms of behaviour as appropriate means of expression of that state.

We should also have to explain some human behaviour in terms of one or other sort of misinformed or irrational plan of action.

Some but by no means all of the theoretical models of unit acts would include as means or conditions of the act the behaviour of other persons. A sociological explanation of the behaviour of these other persons consists in showing that it has a place in terms of the model of the unit act. It should be noticed that though there may be a valid explanation of the behaviour of these other persons in terms of their own motivation, the relevant point for the sociologist is the role which their behaviour plays in terms of the scheme of action of the hypothetical actor with which the model starts.

The model may further be used to explain the behaviour of still further persons C, which serves as means for the action of B, whose behaviour is an essential means for the hypothetical actor A. It also serves to explain the various norms, controls and sanctions which induce B or C to behave in the required ways.

Finally once a pattern of behaviour is established as necessary for the various parties, we should regard as explained for sociological purposes (a) any system of economic allocation which assigned to the different parties the facilities appropriate to their part in the total pattern of interaction (b) any system of power distribution whose effect was to prevent any violation of the system of economic allocation (c) any system of ultimate values which asserted the legitimacy of this system of power distribution and (d) any religious beliefs and ritual which had the effect of causing adherence to this system of ultimate values.

If, however, we started with the more complex case of social conflict (i.e. where B does not do what A wishes) we should regard as explained for sociological purposes any conflict in the economic, political, value or religious sphere in which the two sides to the conflict fitted in with A's and B's needs for facilities, power, legitimation and supernatural support. Such is the case for instance with the Marxist model for the analysis of capitalist societies. Starting with the notion of a conflict of purpose between capitalist and workers it goes on to explain the conflicts in the legal, political, ideological and religious 'superstructure'.

It will be seen that models of this kind can be used in all cases to replace the functionalist organic model discussed in the previous chapter. The difference is that the point of ultimate reference of the explanations which they yield is clear and unambiguous in a way in which the category of the 'needs of the social structure' is not. Moreover the possibility of concealed value judgements is excluded since the necessity of any behaviour explained is explicitly stated to depend upon a particular sort of unit act being necessary. If circumstances change and this unit act is no longer necessary, then none of the behaviour explained in terms of it is necessary. And if anyone takes moral objection to any such behaviour, he is not bound to accept it as inevitable (which is suggested by the functionalist model) but may consider whether the system as a whole may be changed by eliminating the original unit act.

Having now gone some way towards clarifying the nature of sociological explanations employing the action frame of reference, we may now go on to discuss some of the problems which arise from the relationship between the model of the stable social system and the model of social conflict. First we will consider further the problem of the role of values in social systems and then go on to an analysis of the problems involved in explaining social change.

VI

VALUES IN SOCIOLOGICAL
THEORY

POSITIVISM, IDEALISM AND VOLUNTARISM

THE analysis of sociological explanations in the foregoing
chapters leads to conclusions which conflict somewhat,
not merely with the functionalism of the anthropologists, but with the 'structural functionalist' approach which
Talcott Parsons has used in his later work. Because so much of
what has already been said about systems of action and interaction depends upon Parsons' own ideas, it is now necessary to
discuss the points at which the approach to sociology here
suggested differs from that which he advocates. The crux of the
matter turns on the question of the role which we assign to
values in social systems.

Parsons' first great contribution to sociological thought was
contained in his book *The Structure of Social Action*, a work
without parallel as an analytical history of sociological thought.
In this he deals with the work of the great European sociologists,
Pareto, Durkheim and Weber, and with the economic theory of
Alfred Marshall, and seeks to show that each in one way or
another was trying to find a way of transcending the limitations
of utilitarianism and idealism in solving the 'Hobbesian
Problem of Order'. The essence of their problem was that of
finding an appropriate place for values in their conceptualization of interaction and social systems.

Utilitarianism, as Parsons sees it, was one among several
'positivist' attempts to develop a theory of action. By a theory
of action Parsons says that he means, 'any theory the empirical

96

reference of which is to a concrete system, which may be considered to be composed of the units here referred to as unit acts'.[1] A unit act has the following 'minimum characteristics':—
'(1) an end, (2) a situation, analyzable in turn into (a) means and (b) conditions and (3) at least one selective standard in terms of which the end is related to the situation'.

Positivistic systems of action treat 'scientifically valid empirical knowledge as the actor's sole theoretically significant mode of subjective orientation to his situation'.

That is to say that the actor is assumed to have a full scientist's knowledge of the elements in his situations, to draw conclusions 'scientifically' from this knowledge, and to act as an applied scientist might wish. There is thought to be no other 'theoretically significant' relationship between an actor and his situation, though there may be certain elements which are not theoretically significant but random. Some positivist theories allow for such random elements; others do not. Utilitarianism is distinguished from other forms of positivism by the fact that it does. Especially it recognizes ends as being random factors.

But once it has accepted that ends are not subject to scientific prediction or control (in Bentham's phrase 'Pushpin is as good as poetry') it confines itself to the analysis of action in terms of elements which are. As Parsons says, ends are admitted only as 'data for the empirical application of the theoretical system'.[2] We cannot predict ends, but given the ends, utilitarianism claims that the scientific orientation of the actor is sufficient to explain his conduct.

Parsons also gives a number of other cases of positivistic theories. In practice the one of major interest is that in which factors are recognized as influencing the course of human behaviour away from the rational scientific pursuit of ends, but these are treated merely as causative factors over which the actor has no control. As Parsons puts it again and again, action is explained in terms of the natural science categories of heredity and environment. When Parsons speaks of utilitarian explanation breaking down into radical positivism he seems to have in mind the introduction of explanations in terms of heredity and environment for those factors not explicable in terms of the utilitarian scheme.

The crucial feature of all positivist theories of action, however,

[1] Parsons, *The Structure of Social Action*, p. 77.   [2] *Ibid.*, p. 82.

is that they have no place at all for 'normative elements'. These they tend to explain away by assimilating them to the category of conditions, or to treat as random and theoretically irrelevant elements. At the opposite extreme are idealistic theories in which the normative elements are the only ones and the element of 'conditions' and that of the 'rational scientific' orientation of the actor disappears. As Parsons says: 'In an idealistic theory action becomes a process of "emanation" of "self-expression" of ideal or normative factors. Spatio-temporal phenomena become related to action only as modes of expression or embodiments of meanings".[1]

Parsons own view is that an adequate theory of social action must be a 'voluntaristic' theory which allows a place to both normative and 'conditional' elements. This much is quite consistent with the view expounded in the previous chapter. What we referred to there for convenience as 'ritual rules' are normative elements in Parsons' sense. So also are the ultimate values in terms of which power in a social system is declared to be legitimate. But beyond this, points of disagreement between our approach and that of Parsons arise. For although we may argue with Parsons that normative elements enter into the sort of unit act which occurs in social systems, this by no means implies that social systems are completely integrated by such elements. And this is the point to which Parsons' thought continually seems to be moving, even in *The Structure of Social Action*, but much more obviously in *The Social System*.

It will be remembered that the central point of Parsons' interest in his earlier work is 'the Hobbesian problems of order'. He uses the term 'Hobbesian' here, because he rightly saw that Hobbes faced up to the implications of the assumptio n of unrestrained hedonistic individualism among human beings much more boldly than did the Utilitarians. Hobbes saw that enlightened self-interest had no place within the utilitarian system and therefore had to suggest that the solution to the problem of order must come from outside the system. Parsons' view is that there is no solution of the problem at all if the utilitarian assumptions are accepted and he uses his analysis of the development of Durkheim's thought to show that alternative assumptions might be made.

[1] *Ibid.*, p. 82.

DURKHEIM ON THE FORMS OF SOCIAL SOLIDARITY

Durkheim's first major work *The Division of Labour* was explicitly designed as an attack on the utilitarianism of Herbert Spencer. He rejected Spencer's view that human society could be understood as the product of contracts entered into for reasons of self-interest between a number of selfish individuals. Against Spencer he pointed out the idea of a pre-contractual and non-contractual element underlying contract, a form of social solidarity, which though it differed sharply from the social solidarity of primitive societies, was a form of social solidarity nevertheless.

However, Durkheim's position was explicitly positivistic. He spoke of treating 'the facts of the moral life by the method of positive science'. Hence, although in his treatment of the 'mechanical solidarity' of primitive societies, he gropes after a conception of norms and collectively held ends, his account of the organic solidarity of complex societies leads him to the conclusion that it is caused by something like population pressure. This, as Parsons says, is essentially a biological factor.

Perhaps, however, Parsons makes too much of this in his desire to exhibit the various temptations by which positivism attracts the best sociologists away from voluntaristic theories. There are two other points about Durkheim's treatment of social solidarity in complex societies which deserve at least equal attention and which seem to indicate his acceptance of normative elements as having a place there. Firstly, as Parsons admits, the 'conscience collective' underlying mechanical solidarity clearly does include normative elements and the secondary account of the origins of organic solidarity which Durkheim gives is that it follows from the 'progressive inter-determination of the conscience collective'. In other words, whereas the collective conscience in simple social conditions lays down immediate ends and detailed means for achieving them, in more complex conditions it sets only more generalized ends and leaves the individual free to choose the intermediate means. Thus in both cases the notion of the collective conscience is used to attack the utilitarian conception that the ends of an individual in a social system can be purely random.

But secondly there is another notion which is implicit in Durkheim's view of organic solidarity as revealed in his analysis of the anomic forms of the Division of Labour and which becomes important in Durkheim's later work. This is the idea of a guild society. The sort of social solidarity which is produced by the division of labour is one in which particular ends are set for each occupation, but these ends are all the means for the attainment of more ultimate values, by means of which the activities of each individual or occupation are integrated into the social system. By contrast, if the division of labour is pushed beyond a certain point either in industry or science, or if the interests of capital and labour are not harmonious, Durkheim tells us that we are dealing with a case of the anomic division of labour.

Thus organic solidarity turns out to be a state of affairs in which the happiness of the individual is bound up with seeking ends which are integrated with those of other individuals. The same notion is implicit in Durkheim's discussion of 'anomie' in 'Suicide'.[1] Anomic suicide occurs when the individual is left free to seek ends without limit. The natural state of a social system by contrast is one in which he finds happiness by seeking the limited ends which society sets for him. All this, of course, suggests the guild society of the mediaeval town and it is not surprising that in his political writing Durkheim writes as a guild socialist.[2]

Now this recognition of the integration of society through the pursuit of complementary ends is not the only point at which Durkheim introduces normative elements into his system. He recognizes rules of a non-scientific character (equivalent to our ritual rules) both in his writings on social control and in his *Elementary Forms of Religious Life*. Thus, in addition to ends being normatively controlled, we find that the means may not be simply the appropriate scientific means but means laid down by a norm. Further Durkheim discusses both the relationship between norms and needs (the emphasis in his later work being more and more on the internalization of norms, until in *The Elementary Forms of Religious Life* he declares 'Society can only exist in and through the individual'), and also the relations between norms and symbols.

Our purpose here is not to discuss these developments in

---

[1] Durkheim, *Suicide* (1952).

[2] *See* Durkheim, *Professional Ethics and Civic Morals* (1957) and *Socialism and Saint-Simon* (1959).

Durkheim's thought in any detail. It suffices to note that he introduces normative elements which have no place in a utilitarian or other positivist systems at the level of the ends which actors pursue, at the level of the means they use and at the personality level. We need have no quarrel with this. What is much more questionable, however, is the assumption that these norms taken as a whole constitute some sort of social consensus which served to integrate all unit-acts into a system. If this were the case, there would be little room left for the rational-scientific, the conditional and the random elements with which Durkheim started. He would have ended up with an idealistic theory of action.

Now Parsons sees that Durkheim's final position in *The Elementary Forms of Religious Life* is idealistic in this sense. Indeed it is quite dramatically so. For having started from a positivist position of assuming that all the elements of the actor's orientation to his situation must be comprehensible by the methods of positive science, in his chapters on epistemology, Durkheim argues that even the categories of space, time and causation are derivable from social or normative sources.[1] But Parsons treats this as an aberration and holds that the main tendency of Durkheim's work was towards a voluntaristic theory including the factors apart from the normative. If we are correct, however, from the very beginning in *The Division of Labour*, Durkheim's search for a type of social solidarity underlying contract led him in an idealist direction.

The curious feature of *The Division of Labour* is the assumption that societies based upon the 'anomic division of labour' are not really societies at all. Either this, or we must assume that Durkheim's object is not that of an empirical scientist at all, but that of a social reformer making recommendations. But if we are to treat *The Division of Labour* as a guide to empirical study, we are bound to object that societies in which occupational roles are not integrated, and in which the interests of capital and labour conflict, do really exist. Indeed far from being abnormal in the statistical sense, societies which have these features have been characteristic of Europe at least since the Reformation. Durkheim's analysis of organic solidarity seems to apply nowhere outside the mediaeval towns.

If this is the case, we seem to be back where we started, so far

[1] Durkheim, *Elementary Forms of the Religious Life* (1915), Conclusion.

101

as the analysis of industrial society is concerned. Durkheim's 'organic solidarity' seems to be an inadequate model and we are left with Hobbesian or utilitarian theory. But is this really the only alternative? Is the problem posed correctly by Parsons in the first place? He presents us only with two stark alternatives. Either we have social order or we have Hobbes' war of all against all.

THE OTHER ALTERNATIVES TO HOBBES

There are, however, at least two other alternatives. One is that, though there might be some sort of relative order in which although major conflicts are avoided, there are areas in which self-interest operates and in which rival norms clash. The other is that, although every man is not against his neighbour, the society is divided into two or more groups with conflicting aspirations. Such groups may be bound together within themselves by normative elements, but these norms serve to unite them for conflict with opposing groups. This clearly is the kind of model of modern industrial society suggested by Marx. There is room for normative elements in a Marxist type theory. Indeed they are quite essential to any account of the development of class-solidarity. But a conflict of interests or ends is put at the centre of the model of the system as a whole. The result of this is that the model is directly applicable to the kind of social system which we find in industrial society. Such systems do not have to be treated in an appendix as abnormal, as is the case with Durkheim's *Division of Labour*.

The correctness or otherwise of Marx's two-class model is not at issue here. What we wish to draw attention to is the fact that short of a war of all against all, there is the possibility that the ends which men pursue in a social system may not be fully integrated, and that there may be a clash of interests and ultimate values in a social system which divides participants in that system into hostile factions. The relevance of emphasizing normative elements then lies in the fact that they help us to explain how individuals subordinate their own private interests to those of the group or class.

There is also another point at which norms are apparently important. This is that conflicts between groups tend to be projected on to an ideological level. But it should not be supposed that they are simply appealing to a common value system which governs the actions of all groups. In such an ideological battle the object of any group is to represent its own actions as consistent with, and the actions of other groups as inconsistent with, certain norms which the other group is known to accept. But the actions of the first group will not be determined by the norms to which it makes appeal. They will be determined by the realistic interests of the group.

C. Wright Mills argues that it is this sort of situation which Parsons is really dealing with and that he mistakes it for a situation of social consensus. Thus he writes:—

'Now, what Parsons and other grand theorists call "value orientation" and "normative structure" has mainly to do with the master symbols of legitimation. This is, indeed, a useful and important subject. The relation of such symbols to the structure of institutions are among the most important problems of social science. Such symbols, however, do not form some autonomous realm within a society; their social relevance lies in their use to justify or oppose the arrangement of power and the position within this arrangement of the powerful. Their psychological relevance lies in the fact that they become the basis for adherence to the structures of power or for opposing it'.[1]

There are, of course, other aspects of 'value orientations' and 'normative structure' than this, but the one to which Wright Mills draws attention is important and we shall return to it when we discuss the theory of conflict and social change. Meanwhile we have to consider the way in which Parsons develops his own theory of social interaction in *The Social System*.

PARSONS' ANALYSIS OF INTERACTION

The starting point of this work is Parsons' microcosmic analysis of the interaction situation. Interaction, he tells us, is always 'doubly contingent'. That is to say that the interaction is not completely determined by the motivation of one of the parties, but depends upon the action of 'alter' fitting in with the expectations of 'ego'. How, then, is it possible for this double contingency to be overcome? According to Parsons:— 'The

---

[1] C. Wright Mills, *The Sociological Imagination* (1959), p. 37.

H

problem of order, and thus the nature of the integration of stable systems of social interaction, that is, of social structure ... focuses on the integration of the motivation of actions with the normative cultural standards which integrate the action system . . .'[1]

This integration of motivation with cultural standards is accomplished by what Parsons calls a two-fold process of 'binding in'. 'Alter' will have internalized the standard or required form of behaviour so that it fits in with his own pattern of need-fulfilment and he will find that 'ego's' approval is dependent upon his conformity.

But, of course, this degree of integration is not always achieved. As Parsons says:—

'The institutionalization of a set of role-expectations and of corresponding sanctions is clearly a matter of degree. This degree is a function of two sets of variables; on the one hand those affecting the actual sharedness of the value-orientation patterns, on the other, those determining the motivational orientation or commitment to the fulfilment of the relevant expectations'.[2]

Thus, there is the possibility that the patterns will not be shared or that the binding in of the patterns with alters motivation will not have been achieved. Complete 'institutionalization' of the action elements is a polar case only and at the other pole is anomie. Parsons himself says:— 'The polar antithesis of full institutionalization is anomie, the absence of structional complementarity of the interaction process or, what is the same thing, the complete breakdown of normative order in both senses'.[3]

Yet having said this Parsons dismisses it on the grounds that it is a 'limiting concept which is never descriptive of a concrete social system' and goes on to discuss the case of complete institutionalization.

But the fact is that both the case of complete institutionalization and the case of complete anomie are limiting concepts. An empiricist sociologist would dismiss both of them and equally a sociologist interested in conceptual analysis and theory would feel justified in developing both concepts further. We should say that Parsons is quite entitled to concentrate on

---

[1] Parsons, *The Social System*, p. 36.
[2] *Ibid.*, p. 39. [3] *Ibid.*, p. 39.

developing the theory of one polar type, but it would be made clear at this point that his sociological theory is branching off in an analytically specialized direction. The other branch of sociological theory would lead to the study of social conflict. Having noted this, we may go on to consider the way in which Parsons treats the normative elements in his system.

THE NORMATIVE ELEMENTS

The main point to be noticed about Parson's work at this point is that the range of his interest in various sorts of normative integrative elements is much narrower than it was in *The Structure of Social Action*. In his analysis of Durkheim's development in that book he had drawn attention to several different points at which systems of action become normatively integrated. There was the possibility of shared or complementary ends, the possibility of the means of action being governed by norms, and also the possibility of the internalization of norms so that compliance becomes a need of the actor. The curious feature of *The Social System* is that the first of these is not discussed. All attention is focused on the value patterns governing the 'orientation' of one actor to another, and ends as such seem to disappear from the system.

The argument by which Parsons arrives at the crucial normative elements in his social system are complex and not always clear, and we cannot hope to reproduce them here. But the following is the broad outline of the argument:—

Firstly there are three aspects of motivation, the cognitive, which is concerned with knowing the facts of the situation, the cathectic, which is concerned with the actors desiring certain objects, and thirdly the evaluative, which is concerned with judging situational elements in terms of some value standard. Secondly the evaluative standards may be rules applying to problems of cognition, cathection or to the integration of action, in this last case either through the integration of the acts of one individual in terms of a personality system or the acts of more than one individual in terms of a system of inter-action.

Thirdly in any complete human action, since all of the above elements are involved, differentiation must take place in terms of the primacy of one or other of the evaluative elements.

Action may be instrumental, in which case the main standards which are applied are those relating to the correct means of knowing and understanding the world. It may be 'expressive' in which the main type of standard applied is that concerned with the appropriate symbolism to express a 'need-disposition'. Or it may be moral in which case the standards applied will be those concerned with achieving integration either of the personality or the 'collectivity'.

What Parsons seems to be doing here is to revive his differentiation of the elements of action expounded in *The Structure of Social Action* in a more complex form. A theory which concentrated solely on instrumental action would be, in terms of the earlier book, a utilitarian system, and a theory which concentrated on the moral elements would be an idealistic system. It is not clear whether there is any parallel between a theory emphasizing expressive action-orientation and the theories of the earlier book. Possibly this represents a later development of Parsons' thought. But clearly a theory which finds a place for all three types of action orientation in Parsons' scheme would be what he had earlier called a voluntaristic theory.

Yet *The Social System* does not in fact rest upon all three types of 'evaluative action-orientation'. It is concerned almost solely with the 'collectivity integrative sub-type of the moral type of evaluative action-orientation' (to use Parsons' own term). It is through the patterning of social systems in terms of these elements that their integration takes place and the other evaluative standards, which might be applied to action by the actor and used as explanations by the sociologist, tend to drop into the background. Parsons may not, it is true, 'have shot clean over into idealism', which is what he accuses Durkheim of doing, but he does concentrate on 'collectively integrative' norms to an extent which makes his system in effect not unlike an idealist one.

Thus we find that in his emphasis in his schematic outline of the elements of action he does again what he did in his microcosmic analysis of the interaction situation. In both cases he sets out a range of possibilities but he goes on to develop a particular one of them only. It is therefore evident that some compensating development of other possibilities is necessary before Parsons' theory can be realistically applied to actual sociological explanation.

But the range of Parsons' interest is even further narrowed when he comes to describe the content of the collectively-integrative elements. What Parsons is interested in here is the moral elements of 'evaluative action orientation' taken by themselves. This means excluding any reference to the content and the ends of action and concentrating on the orientation of one actor to another. The crucial 'collectivity integrative' element turns out to be 'role-expectations'. And as Parsons says about these:—

> To develop a systematic scheme of points of reference, it is . . .
> . . . essential first to analyze those basic or alternatives of selection which are particularly significant in defining the character of re-lations to a social object, and which are constitutive of the character of the relationship pattern itself rather than on its 'content' in interest terms, its cultural or motivational aspects in any sense other than as constitutive of relational patterns.[1]

The value patterns governing the behaviour of one actor to another are the standards in terms of which individuals choose between a number of pairs of alternatives. These are:—

1. The choice between regarding the relationship with the other individual as an end in itself or as a means to some ulterior purpose. This is called the choice between Affectivity and Affective Neutrality.
2. The choice between regarding the other actor as the provider of many services or looking to him for specialized services only. This is called the choice between Diffuseness and Specificity.
3. The choice between regarding oneself as acting only in one's own interests or acting on behalf of a group. This is called the choice between collectivity-orientation and self-orientation.
4. The choice between treating individuals as individuals or regarding them in the role which they play as members of classificatory groups (e.g. producers, consumers, graduates, etc.). This is called the choice between universalism and particularism.
5. The choice between responding to the other individual in terms of what he is and responding to him in terms of

---

[1] *Ibid.*, p. 58–59.

what he has achieved. This is called the choice between Ascription and orientation to achievement.[1]

THE FORMALISM OF PARSONS' APPROACH

The first thing to notice about this classification of alternatives of role expectation is its formal character. One might have thought that a crucial element in role-expectations was the expectation of some specific service by 'alter' in order to achieve in some cases at least a specific end for 'ego'. To put this concretely, I go to my barber to have a shave and a haircut in order to please my family and employers. A social system might be thought of as built up of patterns of motivation and 'role-expectation' of this sort. But, focusing his attention narrowly on the formal aspects of my relationship with the barber, Parsons comment would be that my relationship with him is Affectively Neutral and Specific.

The problem here is what we want sociology to do. Is its aim to classify social systems only in the most general formal terms, or does it wish to distinguish between systems in more detail and taking account of the rich variety of their content? The former task is one, of course, to which other great sociologists prior to Parsons have addressed themselves, notably Durkheim and Tönnies. And Parsons has said that his pattern-variables are essentially an attempt to spell out some of the analytical differences between Tönnies' concepts of 'Gemeinschaft' and 'Gesellschaft'. But this may be only the preliminary task for the sociologist and it may be that what we should note about particular relations is not only the fact that alter is or is not regarded as a means to the attainment of an ulterior purpose, but what this ulterior purpose is; not only the fact that specific or defined services are expected, but what these services are.

One reason why this latter approach is to be preferred is that it is only when we know the content as well as the form of what is expected of a role, that we can judge whether it is compatible with the ends of the actor of whom it is expected. Only then can we see whether the situation is an integrated one or one which contains elements of conflict. Parsons, of course, tells us that he is concerned with the case of the completely institutionalized

---

[1] See the section entitled 'The Pattern Alternatives of Value Orientation as Definitions of Relational Role Expectation Patterns.' *Ibid.*, pp. 58–67.

social relation, and he assumes that there is a minimum level of need-satisfaction achieved by the individuals participating in a social system. If we wish to include in sociology an account of those social systems in which participants are relatively dissatisfied with the level of need satisfaction allowed by the existing network of social relations, we should have to take account of the ends which these participants set themselves.

However, it is worth noting that the boundary between formal sociology and a sociology which takes account of the content of action and social relations is not a rigid one. Simmel, who argued that sociology was concerned with the form of social relations without reference to their purpose, nevertheless, saw fit to write about *The Philosophy of Money*,[1] and it is a matter of argument whether the pursuit of monetary gain is a formal or a substantive element in social systems. And if we are to be concerned with large-scale social systems, the ultimate end to which all activities are referred for explanation might well be the attempt of certain individuals to live in accordance with a formal and abstract philosophy of life. Thus, Weber, who did seek to explain social systems in terms of the ends sought by individuals, explained the structure of capitalist society in terms of the Calvinist ethic. And the main features of this Calvinist ethic and of the social structure which it produced was a rationalism of conduct roughly equivalent to Parsons' Affectively Neutral, Specific, Universalist, Achievement-Oriented type of relationship.

Nevertheless not all social systems can be thought of as determined by a philosophy of life in this way. Weber himself was writing about the origins of capitalism and as Tawney for instance has shown the philosophy of life of early capitalism did gradually give way over the centuries to a much cruder search for profit. It might be argued, of course, that this search for profit itself demanded a high degree of rationalization in every area of life. But the proletariat have not behaved as so many 'alters' in a sociological scheme. They have pursued their own ends and have produced the socialist movement, which though it has perpetuated many bureaucratic features of capitalism, nonetheless has been marked by strong elements of an affective, diffuse, particularistic, ascriptive kind.

---

[1] Simmel, *Philosophie des Geldes* (1900).

NORMS AND THE BALANCE OF POWER

It is true, of course, that patterns of social relations do not always entirely fit in with the interest which men pursue. Thus industrialization is sometimes inhibited by the survival of a 'gemeinschaft' mentality among a people which lingers on as a habit. Thus we might admit that to some extent the value-system of the society in the sense in which Parsons writes of it is an independent variable of which we must take account. But Parsons goes much further than this. For him the interests which can be pursued and the facilities which are available for use by particular individuals and classes are dependent upon the value system in operation.

Thus we are told that 'every social system must have mechanisms for the allocation of possession of facilities, because their possession is desirable and they are inherently limited in supply relation to demand'. And the sources of this scarcity apart from the fact that there simply are not enough to go round in some cases are said to be relational. But what this means is that some people have more power than others.

Now we might expect this to lead to a discussion of the struggle for power in social systems. But in Parsons the discussion does not take this course. The scarcity of facilities imposed by the unequal distribution of power is something to which the social system has to be adapted and the value patterns ensure the perpetuation of a particular system of allocation of facilities and power. Thereafter discussion of power drops into the background and the system is discussed as though it were integrated purely in terms of value-patterns.

There is a very important point here. If we had started our analysis of social systems by positing some measure of rejection by 'alter' of 'ego's' expectations and hence some measure of conflict, it would have been obvious that to some extent ego would try to compel alter to conform to his expectations. It would also have been obvious that alter's eventual behaviour would have been determined by the sort of balance of power prevailing. No doubt the more fortunate party would also have produced moral rationalizations of the situation. But the actual situation would have been produced not by a normative system, but by the balance of power and the eventual agreement of the parties.

110

Thus, even if it is admitted that social integration is in part dependent upon value systems, there is also a substructure to social order which is determined by the struggle for power and the balance of power. Any complete account of a social system must describe the nature of this power. Moreover, as Wright Mills has pointed out, there are many transitional points between actual coercion and legitimate rule or rule by consent. For 'among the means of power that now prevail is the power to manage and manipulate the consent of men'.[1] No doubt sociologists will always show their bias here and what one calls 'manipulation' another will call 'consent to common norms'. But the point to notice about Parsons is precisely that, in subordinating the questions of power to the question of normative order, he shows a markedly conservative bias.

The practical implications of this point are clearly illustrated in a field such as that of industrial sociology. Anyone with experience of industrial relations knows that the actual relations prevailing between employers and employees are determined by a contract which ends a period of negotiations in which both sides are likely to deploy their power in threatening strikes and lock-outs. Yet very often industrial sociology ignores all this and discusses the social relations of a factory, as though they were akin to those of village community, in terms of some sort of value system which is supposed to be accepted by both sides.

Of course there are some fields of sociological study like industrial sociology where the power element in social relations is far more evident than in other cases. But we quote this extreme case in order to emphasize that the pursuit of ends which, from the point of view of the system as a whole, are 'random', does go on, and that if the pursuit of these ends finds no sanction in the norms of the society it may yet continue and be backed by force instead of moral or social authority. And between the sanction of force and that of the social norms there are many intermediate points.

We need not return to a Hobbesian or a utilitarian position in order to say this. What we are asserting is the need for a theory such as Parsons suggested which avoids the pitfalls of both positivism in its various forms on the one hand and idealism on the other. By concentrating solely on the normative

[1] C. Wright Mills, *Op. cit.*, p. 40.

aspects of action Parsons produces a theory which is differentiated from idealism only by the fact that he recognizes that the norms affect human conduct only voluntarily, that is to say that they may or may not be obeyed. But once he has shown that they are subjectively experienced in a different way from other factors, he goes on to describe these norms as though they were themselves the social structure.

What we want is a theory which finds a place for both normatively oriented action and action which can be understood as governed by something like scientific knowledge of the relation between means and ends. We also need to recognize that some of the ends which the actors in our system pursue may be random ends from the point of view of the system or actually in conflict with it. If there is an actual conflict of ends, the behaviour of actors towards one another may not be determined by shared norms but by the success which each has in compelling the other to act in accordance with his interests. Power then becomes a crucial variable in the study of social systems.

THE OUTLINES OF A CONFLICT MODEL OF SOCIAL SYSTEMS

The most useful way to conclude this chapter will be to set out the main lines of model which would be useful in analyzing the sort of modern industrial society with which we have most frequently to deal, and showing the place that values have in that model. In the first place we should seek to show what ends were pursued by individuals and groups within the society. It would then become evident that we were faced neither with Hobbes' state of nature nor with a state of perfect harmony. We should find that many members of the society had what MacIver calls like and common interests and that these tend to form up into groups. Between the groups there would be a conflict situation. Our model would then seek to describe the structure of the groups and the relations between them.

Looking first at the structure of the separate groups we should expect to find some commonly accepted definition of the group's aims, to achieving which the actions of individual members would be directed. Many of these actions could be directly understood as means to the achievement of the group's end (i.e. 'appropriate' means as defined by empirical science).

Other actions and relationships might not have this direct relationship to the group's aims and might be subjectively experienced as normatively controlled by the members. They might, however, have an indirect relationship through the contribution which they make to group solidarity, i.e. to the prevention of internal conflict. We should also allow for the fact that certain acts might be related to the group ends not as the scientifically appropriate means but as appropriate in terms of what we called 'ritual rules' of the group. These might be derived from the mythology and ideology of the group. We mention these actions as a separate category from those which contribute to group solidarity, even though they may be the same actions, because it has to be shown empirically that they have this effect. In any case there would be two separate points to be made, firstly that there are certain actions which are related to the group's ends in ways other than those which were deemed appropriate in the light of scientific knowledge, and secondly that these actions contributed to group solidarity.

In describing the group situation we should include the formal aspect of role-expectations in the social relations among individuals. But we should also describe the content of the group-roles. The object of the group-model as a whole would be to show the connection between actions, roles and relations of group members and the group's aims.

As between groups, we should first make clear the points of conflict in their separate aims. We might find that the conflict was a total one or we might find that there were areas of agreement including agreement as to how the conflict might be carried on. But, given that there was a conflict of aims, we should expect each group to seek to enforce upon the other behaviour which at worst did not interfere with and at best actually promoted the achievement of its own aims. If each group did this there would be some sort of power contest using various forms of power and some sort of conflict would ensue until each side recognized that compliance to a certain degree was more profitable than a continuance of the conflict. Provided the balance of power remained stable after agreement had been reached the agreement might be elaborated to provide agreed norms for the behaviour of the members of both groups. But it is also possible that only an uneasy compromise might be arrived at, in which case both sides would remain prepared for

113

a resumption of the conflict. In this case the norms of each separate group might remain unaffected by the truce.

One would also expect that during a period of conflict or truce an ideological battle would continue. Even where conflict is total, there are nearly always common traditions to which appeal can be made and the aim of the ideological argument would be to show that the groups aims were more consistent with the common traditions than those of its opponents. But this is not necessarily to say that the groups in conflict actually have shared values. They may have. But the sole reason for the survival of the common tradition may be that it is necessary for the conduct of the ideological battle.

Thus an alternative model for the analysis of social systems, which includes rational scientific as well as normatively oriented action, and conflict as well as consensus, is perfectly possible without our slipping back into the oversimplifications of positivism which Parsons rightly criticizes. Parsons' own model involves a continually narrowing focus of interest, first on the normative elements of social systems, secondly on the special case of complete integration or 'institutionalization" and, thirdly on the formal aspects of the norms. As a specialized study of one analytically separable element of social systems it has real value. But for the analysis of modern industrial societies and plural societies brought into being by culture contacts it is quite inadequate. For these, the main areas of interest of modern sociology, a model which gives a greater place to action of a rational-scientific kind and to conflict is essential. Hence in the next chapter we turn in greater detail to the theory of social conflict and change.

VII

THE THEORY OF SOCIAL
CONFLICT AND CHANGE

THE idea of 'conflict' has increasingly preoccupied sociologists and anthropologists in the last few years, both on the theoretical and empirical level. On the theoretical level this is indicated by a revival of interest in the writings of Simmel and in the work of Coser who has based his own theories on those of Simmel.[1] Amongst anthropologists, Gluckman has emphasized the role of conflict in primitive societies.[2] And recently Dahrendorf has produced an account of class conflict in industrial societies, which, while revising Marx, stands with Marx in insiting on relating the concept of 'class' to that of conflict.[3] He also explicitly takes issue with Parsons and insists on the need for a conflict model to supplement, if not to replace, Parsons' model of the stable social system.

It may be doubted, however, whether any of the writers mentioned have really taken their criticisms of 'integrationist' and 'functionalist' theory far enough. The point of view from which they have made their criticisms is indicated by Coser's title *The Functions of Social Conflict*, a title which implies the point which Coser explicitly makes, namely, that conflict may be studied not as disruptive of social systems but as having a function within those systems. We have suggested a notion of conflict here, however, which *is* disruptive and it is important to try to see how this is related to the notion as it is used by writers like Coser.

[1] Coser, *The Functions of Social Conflict* (1956).
[2] Gluckman, *Custom and Conflict in Primitive Society* (1955).
[3] Dahrendorf, *Class and Class Conflict in an Industrial Society* (1959).

COSER'S ACCOUNT OF THE ROLE OF CONFLICT IN SOCIAL SYSTEMS

Coser himself makes a broad distinction between conflicts which 'do not contradict the basic assumptions upon which the relationship is founded' and conflicts 'in which the contending parties no longer share the basic values upon which the legitimacy of the social system rests'.[1] It is, of course, the latter type of conflict which we have emphasized hitherto. But for the moment it will be of interest to pursue Coser's analysis of the former type.

What he has to say about this is that 'one safeguard against conflict disrupting the consensual basis of the relationship is contained in the social structure itself: it is provided by the institutionalization and tolerance of conflict'.[2] That is to say that part of the expectation of the parties is that certain questions cannot be regarded as settled in advance, but that when they occur the question of how they are to be settled and what sort of behaviour will be permitted will depend upon the sort of balance of power prevailing at the time.

Thus instead of 'institutionalized' social relationships resting, as they do in Parsons' work, entirely upon norms, part of the institutionalization itself may lie in permitting certain issues to be settled on the basis of the outcome of a conflict between the two parties. Indeed, as Coser puts it, the emergence of norms may depend upon the balance of power achieved.

'Conflict', he writes, 'frequently helps to revitalize existent norms; or it contributes to the emergence of new norms. In this sense, social conflict is a mechanism for adjustment of norms adequate to new conditions. A flexible society benefits from conflict because such behaviour, by helping to create and modify norms, assures its continuance under changed conditions'.[3]

In saying this, Coser seems to go far towards saying that the balance of power is the basic factor in social relationships and that the normative structure is a dependent variable. One might well ask, therefore, whether it would not be better to start one's analysis with the balance of power or the conflict of interests which this balance of power is supposed to settle, rather than beginning by assuming the existence of norms. This, in essence, is what we have already proposed and the implications of doing so will be developed later in this chapter.

[1] Coser, *Op. cit.*, p. 151.   [2] *Ibid.*, p. 152.   [3] *Ibid.*, p. 154.

However, a second point about the disruptiveness of social conflict which Coser makes is relevant here. It is that conflicts are more likely to be disruptive in social groups where 'there exists a high frequency of interaction and high personality involvement of the members', than it is in groups 'comprising individuals who participate only segmentally'. The point here is that in actual social systems the existence of a conflict situation in relation to an isolated aim does not necessarily mean that the whole social system will be disrupted by the conflict. But there are social systems in which aims and relationships are not isolated from one another, as, for instance, in the case of small close knit communities and a conflict arising in any particular sphere will be a conflict between whole persons rather than one which can be kept to the matter in hand.

The distinction which Coser makes here appears at first to be a valid one, for there are societies in which relationships are segmented or related to specific ends, which have entirely different problems from those in which relationships are unspecialised and diffuse. And we may agree that, even though there may be a total conflict in a particular segment (i.e. with no element of consensus in the particular relationship) in the former sort of society, this conflict may not necessarily spread and disrupt the whole social system.

However, there is a further distinction to be drawn here. For the different segmental relationships may not be merely arbitrarily or randomly related to one another. There may be some sort of means-ends relationship between them. If this is so there may be a conflict in the dominant or ultimate segment which will spread all the way back along the means-ends chain.

This point is especially relevant in relation to the theories of Dahrendorf who holds that class conflicts occur between those possessing authority and those who do not possess it. Hence there may be class conflicts in any of a number of different institutions (e.g. in industry, in religion, in politics, etc.). Dahrendorf argues that whether or not the class-conflict becomes really disruptive and revolutionary depends upon whether the class conflicts in the separate institutional contexts become superimposed upon one another.

But the trouble with Dahrendorf's analysis is that it simply turns a blind eye to the enormous amount of sociological and historical research which has shown that conflicts do spread from one institutional context to another, because the separate institutions are related to one another as means to ends. One would scarcely have supposed that any sociologist writing in Max Weber's own country could naïvely pose a theoretical situation in which conflicts in the religious sphere had no connection with conflicts in the sphere of economics and industry. For what Max Weber's work shows is that conflicts about religious ideas had implications for economic organisation and his remark that he was considering only one end of a causal chain suggests that he also imagined a reverse relationship as holding.

Both Coser and Dahrendorf, in fact, dwell on a situation which is not by any means, the only theoretical possibility. The alternative to a society in which relationships are unsegmented may not be a society in which a whole lot of segmentary relations vary at random to one another, but one in which the structure of one segmented relation is causally or functionally linked with another. One does not of course have to hold that all relationships fit into a single functional pattern or a single means-end chain. Indeed part of the burden of our argument so far has been that there may be conflicts between parts of the social structure as well as within its segments. But the concept of randomly varying segments is as artificial as the concept of complete functional integration. We should assume that conflicts will spread in segmented societies as much as they do in close-knit unsegmented societies. There might be more personal hatred in the latter type of society, but that is another matter. We are concerned here with the social not the personality system.

This brings us to Coser's third point which is that conflict brings together those who unite against the common enemy and that where there are a whole lot of cross-cutting conflicts in a social system one enemy in relation to one conflict situation may be one's ally in relation to another and hence social solidarity will be ensured. This, of course, depends upon how far it really is true that social life proceeds entirely by way of ad hoc coalitions. The model for Coser's analysis would be the 'log-rolling' system of American Congress politics. But there is also the British two-party system which reflects the fact that British people find that the enemy on one front is also the enemy on others.

It should be noted that Gluckman makes this point also in relation to primitive societies. Possibly it has greater force there since at a primitive level it may be more possible to understand social relations and activities as being directed toward the attainment of a number of discrete ends (although this is by no means the assumption of functionalist anthropology). But there clearly is a limit in every society to the possible combinations of individuals who can be brought into ad hoc coalitions and as a means of ensuring solidarity the principle of coalitions is limited by this fact.

The point which we wish to make here is that in opposing the idea that conflicts must be disruptive, Coser, Gluckman and Dahrendorf have probably all been guilty of an overemphasis in the other direction. It is true, of course, that the simple two-party two-class model is too oversimplified to provide an adequate tool for the analysis particularly of advanced industrial societies. But the theory of coalitions, if we may call it that, underestimates the extent to which conflicts in modern society tend to coalesce, or to come into relation to each other.

The last category of conflicts which Coser mentions are probably of less importance. These are conflicts of a safety-valve type. In these cases, as Coser says, there is 'a displacement of goal in the actor. He need no longer aim at reaching a solution of the unsatisfactory situation, but merely at releasing the tension which arose from it'. This is the case which Parsons discusses in his analysis of deviant behaviour.[1] According to Parsons the failure of 'alter' to conform to ego's expectations might lead to one or two alternatives. Either ego will learn to have new expectations and learn successfully without pathological complications. Or he will develop an ambivalence so that behaviour indicative of various sorts of tension release will be evident, and even the process of bringing ego back into line with society's requirements has to make allowance for this 'letting off steam'. Parsons fails to consider the alternative that ego might persist quite rationally in his original demands without developing any pathological symptoms or ambivalences (an alternative which would lead to really disruptive conflict). But nonetheless no-one would deny that many conflicts take the course which he and Coser suggest and that they are compatible with the maintenance of social order, (even according

[1] Parsons, *The Social System*, Chapter 7.

to Parsons' analysis, in which he suggests various social niches for the ambivalent, the compulsive and the deviant.)

The sociologists of the conflict school have indeed made an important point. Even a structural-functional analysis should allow far more scope for the working-out of conflict situations and Parsons has failed to make such an allowance, except in his analysis of deviance which deals only with the least important 'safety-valve' type of conflict. We should have a far more flexible model for the analysis of complex societies if we allowed for norms which depended in part on a balance of power and for cross-cutting conflicts which led to coalitions sufficiently strong to hold a flexible open society together. But this is by no means to say that these are the only sort of conflicts and we must now turn our attention to the study of conflicts which are disruptive of any sort of total functional interaction in a social system.

CONFLICT IN WEBER, MANNHEIM AND MYRDAL

Curiously the analysis of this sort of conflict emerges, except in the important case of Marx, only as a by-product of a particular methodological tradition. Many writers have noted that objectivity is not possible in the social sciences in the same sense as it is in the natural sciences. But this arises from the fact that social relations and activities can be judged necessary or unnecessary, functional or dysfunctional, according to which of a number of conflicting standpoints they are looked at. And these standpoints may be the standpoints of participant individuals, groups or classes, in the society. Thus we may expect to glean something of importance about disruptive conflicts from those sociologists who have made a serious analysis of the problem of objectivity in social science, especially from Weber, Mannheim and Myrdal.

Weber tells us in his paper on *Objectivity in Social Science* that 'there is no absolutely objective scientific analysis of culture, or put perhaps more narrowly but certainly not essentially differently for our purposes—of social phenomena independent of special and one-sided viewpoints according to which— expressly or tacitly, consciously or unconsciously they are selected, analyzed and organized for expository purposes. The reasons for this lie in the character of the cognitive goal of all

120

research in social science which seeks to transcend the purely formal treatment of the legal or conventional norms regulating life'.[1]

Now in the context in which Weber says this he is referring to the fact that any social activity, institution or relation may be looked at from an economic, a religious, or some other point of view. But it also has two other implications. One is that the conceptual scheme of the sociologist might be affected by the particular value-standpoint which he himself adopts. That is to say that he might be interested in studying what activities are conducive to the attainment of states of affairs which he himself desires. The other is that these activities might be judged according to the contribution which they make to the attainment of the ends of participant actors.

Mannheim, whose position owes much to Marx on the one hand, and to Weber and his predecessors on the other, saw the implications of this latter point. For if sociology is concerned with showing the relationship between activities and the purposes of actors in a social system, there was no such thing as objectivity in the sense of letting the facts speak for themselves. What were necessary facts depended upon from whose point of view you looked at them. From the point of view of one set of actors they might be necessary to the attainment of their ends. But from the point of view of another set they would not be, and hence would be likely to be removed in time.[2]

The same point was made by Myrdal who insisted that there were no simple objective facts about race relations, but only facts in relation to value premises. Our concern, however, is not primarily with the problem of objectivity, to which we shall return, but with that of conflict in social systems and here Myrdal has something of direct importance to say. In talking about the selection of value starting points he says,

> In a scientific treatment of the practical aspects of social problems the alternative sets of hypothetical value premises should not be chosen arbitarily. The principle of selection should be their relevance. Relevance is determined by the interests and ideals of actual persons and groups of persons. There is thus no need of introducing value premises which are not held by anybody.

[1] Weber, *The Methodology of the Social Sciences*, p. 72.
[2] Mannheim, *Ideology and Utopia*. Mannheim's views are discussed in more detail in Chapter 9.

Within the circle of relevance so determined a still more narrow circle of significance may be taken to denote valuations which are held by substantial groups of people or by small groups with substantial social power. Realistic research on practical problems will have to concentrate its attention upon value premises corresponding to valuations which have high social significance or are likely to gain in social significance. On the other hand, it is certainly not necessary to adopt only those value premises which are held by a majority of the population or by a politically dominant group.[1]

Three assumptions which Myrdal makes here should be noted. (1) That there are conflicts of 'value-premises' or as we should say aspirations or aims between groups in American society. (2) That these conflicts are sufficiently radical in scope to affect the structure of the society at almost any point at which we care to study it. (It is because of this that Myrdal insists that we should make our value premises clear in any study of that structure.) (3) That the actual course of events is likely to be determined by the power at the disposal of groups and that the balance of power might change so that particular value premises might gain in social significance. In other words Myrdal takes for granted a conflict model of social systems similar to that which we outlined in the previous chapter and to which we must now return.

THE NATURE OF SOCIAL CONFLICT

(a) The formation of conflict groups

In its simplest form this model starts by assuming two parties with conflicting aspirations or aims. The achievement of these aims in any case requires the co-operation of others in complex chains of interaction and, even if there were basically no conflict situation, a system of social interaction would be necessary for each of the original two parties. The conflict situation, however, gives an additional reason for dependence upon such an interaction system. For in the process of conflict the actors might be expected to look for allies who will add to the strength of the sanctions they can bring to bear against the other side. Allies will be found who have a similar situation and out of the alliances there will emerge groups structured for participation

[1] Myrdal, *Value in Social Theory*, pp. 157–158.

in conflict. At this point it will become possible to speak of aims, aspirations and interests *of the conflict groups*, rather than merely the aspirations and aims of individuals. What these are will depend upon the nature of the conflict situation.

The most basic conflicts will be conflicts over access to the means of life. These may take place within some sort of ordered context where bargaining is the basic form of conflict and conflict ends with some sort of exchange or contract. Or at the other extreme we may have a non-peaceful conflict in which there is no restriction on the drasticness of the means which are used. And in between the two extremes there will be found a number of intermediate stages. The basic situation may appear to be one of peaceful bargaining but the parties may be able through their control of facilities essential to their opponents to force a settlement on their own terms. A point is reached at which this process is hard to distinguish from the open use of violence and the threat of violence.

This is, of course, the basic type of relationship which exists in early industrial societies between the owners and the non-owners of the means of production. The owners require the labour of the non-owners and the non-owners require paid employment in order to be able to purchase the means of existence. Before a bargain is struck each side will attempt to compel acceptance of its terms by denying to the other the use of the facilities which are under its own control. In order to do this, any individual will be forced to organize and combine with other individuals on the same side of the conflict. Hence one would expect the emergence of something like classes in Marx's sense.

The conflict may, on the other hand, be only indirectly connected with access to the means of life. Very often the conflict may be over the control of legitimate power or it may be over the control of ideas. Thus in the history of many countries, the great popular political movements have centred not around the question of employment, but around the question of political independence or the questions of religion and education. But in any case the consequence of the basic conflict situation is the emergence of conflict groups the activities of whose members contribute to the attainment of the group's aims.

It might be the case of course that a conflict could be

confined to one sphere and there is the other possibility raised by Coser of a number of cross-cutting conflicts. But there is also this possibility of a 'two nations' situation emerging. This idea seemed to Disraeli to fit the facts of Victorian Britain and it certainly has its application to-day in the plural societies of Africa. It will be useful therefore to develop the concept theoretically in a pure form in order to see what sort of social structure it implies.

(b) The ruling class situation

The most important point to be made about such a situation is that instead of one set of institutions embracing all the members of the society, we should have two. If the situation was one in which one of the two conflict groups dominated the society, the institutions which served the purposes of that group would be claimed to be the institutions of the social system as a whole. Its members would claim that its property system and the sorts of power which supported it were the legitimate institutions of the society.[1] But the opposing group would deny this claim to legitimacy and would develop its own economic system by devising ways of limiting the power associated with ruling class property, its own political system concerned with mobilizing power to resist the political power of the ruling class and its own religion, myths and educational system whose effect would be to set a new standard of legitimacy.

In the most extreme form the subject group would actually be engaged in the overthrow of the social system of the ruling class. But long before this happens the characteristics of its members would come to be organized into a kind of counter-system to that of the ruling class. This is not to say that none of the activities of its members would have any independent significance. This is not necessarily claimed by those who put forward the model of an integrated social system either. But insofar as there is a social determinant in the behaviour of the members of the conflict group, it would be found in the role played by their behaviour in the total conflict situation and not in the needs of the social system as a whole.

Assuming still a situation in which one group did exercise effective power, one would expect that group to consolidate its

[1] For a detailed discussion of the concept of 'legitimacy' see Weber, *The Theory of Social and Economic Organization*, Chapters 1 and 3.

power by claiming that its power was legitimate. It would make considerable ideological efforts to get this notion accepted by the members of the ruled group. And it might be partially or even wholly successful in this, thus undermining those members' belief in the values of their own group.

It should be noticed that it is in something like this context that Weber discusses the notion of legitimacy. He introduces it in a chapter entitled 'Forms of Imperative Co-ordination', and the way in which he does so indicates that he sees the fact of imperative co-ordination as something which has to be explained. It does not spring spontaneously from the normative consensus of a society. A belief in the legitimacy of an order is the last of a series of reasons for accepting imperative co-ordination and at the other end of the series is sheer acquiescence in the face of superior force.

But this claim to legitimacy is likely to be made more often than it is accepted. In some situations the ruled group may, while being quite unable to revolt effectively, embark on a course of passive resistance, whose whole object is to compel those who rule to back up its demands by the sanction on which it really depends, namely, physical violence. Passive resistance is in essence, simply a denial of a claim to legitimate authority. Or again, although the legitimacy of the position of the ruling class may to some extent be accepted, this is not incompatible with the continuance in other individuals or even in the same individuals of other attitudes which deny it. Thus those who exercise authority within the ruled group will be continuously engaged in an ideological struggle to prevent the encroachment of ruling class values, and even after the ruling class have successfully established their authority there will be a minority who cling to the old values of the days of struggle. In a later chapter we shall see how this affects the question of class-identification in contemporary society.

The ideological battle here referred to takes us a stage further in the development of our conflict model. The first stage was to outline the way in which the separate conflict groups or the two nations could be thought of as emerging. The attempt to establish a legitimate order and its acceptance or rejection by those who are ruled indicates one of the ways in which the groups begin to interact. Wright Mills apparently has some such model as this in mind as the appropriate one for the analysis of contemporary society in the passage which we have already quoted, in which he tells us that the social relevance of the 'master symbols of legitimation' 'lies in their use to justify or to oppose the arrangement of power and the positions within it of the powerful'.

(c) The revolutionary situation

So far, however, we have assumed that the arrangement of power is something fixed and immutable. But this it is certainly not. And for a variety of reasons, as soon as the nature of this power is recognized, it becomes apparent that it must continually change. For the factors involved in the power situation of the dominated group are highly variable factors such as the strength of their aspirations, their capacity for corporate action, their numbers and the degree to which their social role vis-a-vis their rulers becomes indispensible. The strength of the aspirations of such a group will depend upon the effectiveness of indoctrination and the quality of leadership, upon the intensity of their exploitation and upon the example of similar groups in other societies. Their capacity for corporate action will again depend upon leadership and organizing ability as well as on the organizational examples coming from outside the group, including the example of the ruling class.

The other factors are ones which are continuously changing because of advances in technology. Technological changes produce new roles in the social system, give a greater strategic importance to some old roles or increase the number of people in particular situations. This has been true not only with regard to the social institutions connected with production but in other spheres also, for instance, in the field of mass communications and in that of military organizations.

When such changes occur in the balance of power there may be two possible outcomes. Either there will be a complete revolution in the social system or some sort of compromise will be worked out between the classes. If the revolution is complete it will destroy not merely the domination of the ruling class but the very basis of its existence. There is, of course, the possibility that an élite from those who were in subjection might displace the personnel occupying the old ruling class positions and this is a possibility which Pareto made central to his political sociology. But with a real and sudden shift in the balance of power the subject class will find that it cannot make gains commensurate with its new power unless it destroys the basis of the old conflict situation altogether. This is not to say that no new conflicts will develop. They may well do, but around new issues. Thus, for example, the destruction of capitalism may produce a social order in which the old conflict between labour and capital is ended. But new conflicts may develop between the controllers of political and economic power and the rest of the people.

The sort of social order, which a class which has newly won power will introduce, cannot, however, be predicted on the basis of knowledge of their past behaviour and of the sorts of counter-institutions which they had built up. Such behaviour and such counter-institutions had meaning only in relation to the group's interests in the conflict situation. They are irrelevant or meaningless in relation to the problem of a new social order not geared to the conflict situation. Nor can it be predicted from knowledge of the charters and other declarations which were evolved during the subject period to describe the utopias of the future. Such charters are usually written in the most general terms and assert the possibility of fulfilling all the aspirations of the group which were frustrated by the old ruling class, even though these may be incompatible with one another. Both the ideology of the days of struggle and the utopias projected during that time might survive in the new situation and reference might be made to them in the ideological arguments which arise. But the actual values of the new society would have to be hammered out in practice in relation to the new goals which the people set themselves. There is a useful sociological framework here for the analysis of political conflicts in post-revolutionary societies. It would seem to be particularly relevant to the sorts of argument which went on in Stalin's Russia.

(d) The truce situation

The other alternative line of development is that which would occur if the old ruling-class adjusted itself quickly to the new balance of power. In this case the gain of not having to pursue the conflict to its most drastic extremes would outweigh the cost of giving up the possibility of completely attaining the group's goals. Thus Joseph Chamberlain is said to have warned the British middle-classes that they would have to 'pay ransom' if they were to retain some of their privileges.[1] And on the other hand there have been the many politicians of reform who have contented themselves with half-loaves, because they have recognized the high cost of whole-loaves in manpower and effort.

Such compromises made possible the emergence of a value system and of social institutions which are the social institutions of neither class, but belong to the truce situation itself. Marx once claimed that the 10 hours bill was a victory for working class political economy over the political economy of the bourgeoisie, a proposition which has been rejected by some Marxists who see all welfare measures as stratagems of the ruling-class to preserve their privileges intact. But neither of these views is correct. The fact is that the truce opens up a limited area of co-operation between the classes and that the new institutions of welfare belong neither to 'working-class' or 'bourgeois' political economy but to the social system of the truce itself.

Whether the new institutions are capable of development so that they become in effect the institutions of a new unitary society will depend on how long the prevailing balance of power lasts. If it is prolonged a new generation will arise for whom the institutions of conflict are nothing more than a folk-memory. The institutions and values of the truce will be the ones which they have internalized. In this case a stage may be reached in which these institutions acquire a legitimacy in the eyes of the whole population which the old ruling-class institutions never enjoyed, however efficient their priests and public relations men.

However, there is another possibility here also. If the ruling-class have made concessions simply in the face of the counter-vailing power of the masses, the weakening of this power due to the collapse of morale during the truce may lead to the old ruling-class returning to its old patterns of behaviour. Thus it would seem that the co-operation of the truce can only be prolonged if the balance of power on which it depended in the first place is in some measure maintained. This is a similar point in relation to total social systems as Coser made in relation to particular segmental relations, when he said that the possibility of conflict could actually contribute to the strength of the norms.

[1] See Halevy, *A History of the English People*, Vol. 5 (1949).

But there is something of a dilemma here because the maintenance of the balance of power situation depends upon the continued existence of the conflict groups and their values and institutions. Thus for any individual the truce situation continually poses value-conflicts. He must on the one hand co-operate with the other side and on the other he must be prepared to participate in activities which are directed against them. On a psychological level he finds that his attitudes towards them are ambivalent. Hence the truce situation will always be precarious and could only become the basis of a new social order in exceptionally favourable conditions.

THE NATURE OF CONFLICT—SUMMARY

The main lines of our conflict model for the analysis of social systems are now fairly clear. They may be summarized as follows:—

1. Instead of being organized around a consensus of values, social systems may be thought of as involving conflict situations at central points. Such conflict situations may lie anywhere between the extremes of peaceful bargaining in the market place and open violence.

2. The existence of such a situation tends to produce not a unitary but a plural society, in which there are two or more classes, each of which provides a relatively self-contained social system for its members. The activities of the members take on sociological meaning and must be explained by reference to the group's interests in the conflict situation. Relations between groups are defined at first solely in terms of the conflict situation.

3. In most cases the conflict situation will be marked by an unequal balance of power so that one of the classes emerges as the ruling class. Such a class will continually seek to gain recognition of the legitimacy of its position among the members of the subject class and the leaders of the subject class will seek to deny this claim and to organize activities which demonstrate that it is denied (e.g. passive resistance).

4. The power-situation as between the ruling and subject classes may change as a result of changes in a number of variable factors which increase the possibility of successful resistance or actual revolution by the subject class. Amongst

these variable factors are leadership, the strength of the members aspirations, their capacity for organization, their possession of the means of violence, their numbers and their role in the social system proposed by the ruling class.

5. In the case of a dramatic change in the balance of power the subject-class may suddenly find itself in a situation in which it cannot merely impose its will on the former ruling-class, but can actually destroy the basis of that class's existence. New divisions within the revolutionary class may open up, but these may be of an entirely different kind to those which existed in the previous conflict situation.

6. The social institutions and culture of the subject-class are geared to, and explicable in, terms of the class's interest in the conflict situation. So far as its long-term aims are concerned, these tend to be expressed in vague and utopian forms. When the subject-class comes to power its actual practices will still have to be worked out. But it is likely that they will be justified and even affected by the morality of conflict and by pre-revolutionary charters and utopias.

7. A change in the balance of power might lead not to complete revolution, but to compromise and reform. In this case new institutions might arise which are not related simply to the prosecution of the conflict, but are recognized as legitimate by both sides. Such a truce-situation might in favourable circumstances give rise to a new unitary social order over a long period, in which limited property rights and limited political power are regarded as legitimately held by particular individuals. But such situations are inherently unstable because any weakening of the countervailing power of the formerly subject class would lead the former ruling class to resume its old ways and the maintenance of this power could easily encourage the subject-class to push right on to the revolutionary alternative.

These points would appear to provide a useful framework in terms of which many important contemporary social situations might be analyzed. The classification of basic conflict situations, the study of the emergence and structure conflict groups, the problem of the legitimation of power, the study of the agencies of indoctrination and socialization, the problem of the ideological conflicts in post-revolutionary situations and in situations of compromise and truce, the study of the relations between norms and systems of power—all these have their place within it.

The model has been developed, of course, in relation to the study of total social systems and with special emphasis upon their overtly political aspects. But it is by no means without relevance to the design of research into problems of particular institutions and social segments. There are, as Dahrendorf was right to point out, always conflicts or potential conflicts between those exercising authority and those over whom it is exercised whatever the institutional context, and wherever such conflicts occur the model suggested is relevant for at least a partial analysis of the problems of the institutions concerned. Sometimes it may serve to supplement the model of a stable system. On other occasions when the conflict is central to the life of the institution it may actually displace it entirely.

One final point may perhaps be worth making in connection with this model. This is that it in no way displaces the sort of detailed analysis of social organization which we suggested in Chapter Five. In that chapter we suggested that any sort of structural-functional analysis of a social system or sub-system should be ultimately related not simply to something as vague and unexplained as the needs of the system, but to a clearly defined end or aim for the system as a whole. This fits in entirely with the present analysis because this starts by assuming sub-systems organized around such aims and goes on to analyze the relations holding between them. The sort of analysis which we discussed in Chapter Five would be employed here as a means of analyzing the internal structure of the conflict groups.

CONFLICT AND CHANGE

We have devoted almost the whole of this chapter to discussing the question of conflict, rather than that of social change, because the sort of theory of conflict which we have suggested *is* a theory of change. There are, however, one or two further points which should be made in connection with the latter topic.

The first of these is that all forms of functionalist theory as it is usually understood are logically debarred from being able to put forward any sociological theory of change. This is because the whole functionalist effort is devoted to showing why things are as they are. They are as they are because they are demanded by the needs of the social structure. And because the social structure is itself thought of as being something unproblematic, there is no question of its changing. Hence there are only three possibilities of tacking a theory of change on to the theory of stable social systems. All may be stated in terms of the organic analogy.

The first would be a theory of random mutations and natural selection. This has quite rightly not been taken seriously except perhaps by Sumner, partly because the notion of randomness taken by itself is a virtual denial of the applicability of scientific explanations, and partly because it leaves unsolved the question of the standards in terms of which natural selection takes place.

The second alternative rests upon making these standards clear. The analogy with biology suggests at once that the secret is to be found in the notion of adaptation to environment and much sociological writing about change has been concerned with changes in the social system consequent upon changes in the environment of the system. The 'environment' includes not only the physical environment but all those factors which are not explicable in terms of the variables of the system. Thus there have been attempts made to explain change in society as an adaptation of the system to such factors as technological change, culture contact, growing moral sensitivity and many other factors.

What functionalism has difficulty in explaining is change arising within the system itself rather than in the environment. The third application of the biological analogy, however, is an attempt to explain change in these terms. It is the idea that social, like organic systems, may be thought of as 'growing'. This is the one possibility of change within the system that the organic analogy leaves open. The difficulty, however, is that, even in biology itself, growth is not something which is properly understood in general theoretical terms. Parsons makes this point when he says,

> It is quite possible, indeed, common to know that certain processes of change do in fact typically take place under certain conditions without being able to deduce the pattern of the processes and their outcome from knowledge of the laws of the system. It is also possible to have considerable knowledge about variations in conditions and a variety of scientific consequences of such variations for the system. A familiar example of this type of knowledge is knowledge of the outline of the biological cycle. There is, in biological science, no general theory of the life cycle, by which

growth, its cessation at maturity, senescenece and finally death can be systematically explained in terms of general laws.[1]

Thus it does not add anything to our knowledge of the causes of change to describe it in terms of birth, growth, senescence, etc., in the way which such writers as Toynbee do. At least there is no scientific theory of change here. There may be some metaphysical theory implied, but, if we reject this as irrelevant, we are merely back where we started confronted with the *empirical* fact of change.

Nor is the problem solved by those writers who foresake the idea of the organism for that of equilibrium. Many of them have spoken of a 'moving' equilibrium. But this is essentially a contradiction in terms. Either a system is in equilibrium or it is moving from one equilibrium to another. It cannot be both things at the same time. Thus the notion of a moving equilibrium remains as a central paradox in such sociological theory.

The action frame-of-reference provides us with much more scope for the development of a theory of change. For it explicitly includes the notion of ends and hence of a possible conflict of ends. But we should nonetheless be cautious about how much we claim for our conflict theory as a theory of change. In particular we should be cautious about claims which are made about laws of change and development.

The case of Marxist social and political theory is of particular interest here, because it has always taken its stand on the Hegelian point that we should study things in process rather than as static entities. Engels, for instance, speaks of Hegel's 'great basic thought that the world is not to be comprehended as a complex of ready made things, but as a complex of processes in which things apparently stable go through an uninterrupted process of coming into being and passing away'.[2] And, the Hegelian notion of dialectical change becomes even more relevant when we apply it to society than when it is applied in the physical sciences for such change is dialectical in the original sense of the term. The model which we have suggested is based on the idea of an argument, albeit a practical rather than a theoretical one, and it would not be stretching the meaning of the terms too far to identify the proposals for social

[1] Parsons, *The Social System*, p. 487.
[2] Engels, *Ludwig Feuerbach and the End of the Classical German Philosophy* (1955).

organization of one social class as thesis, those of the other as antithesis and the actual outcome of the conflict as synthesis. Marx seems indeed to have shown great insight in identifying the dialectic with the class struggle. Our model sets out in detail the implications of his doing so.

What we have to beware of, however, is the suggestion that knowledge of the thesis and antithesis is sufficient to give us knowledge of what the synthesis must be. Even if we understand the social system of a subject class during the phase of conflict we do not know how it will organize society in a post-revolutionary situation. Therefore it is misleading to use such images as that of the germ of the new society being present in the womb of the old. It is not. All that a revolution settles is that the formerly subject group will be able to create a new social order. It does not entirely settle the question of what that social order will be like.

At the moment, then, all that our theoretical model does is to suggest areas of investigation. We should be concerned to understand the nature of the conflicting interests at the heart of a social system and we should also study the changing balance of power between interest-groups and the ideologies in terms of which their actions are justified in various situations (i.e. where there is a ruling class in power, where there is a truce situation, where there has been a successful revolution and so on). All these factors would be relevant to understanding the new synthesis or social order. But until we have a great deal more empirical material we shall not be able even to begin speculating as to why a particular synthesis emerges from a particular sort of conflict.

Nonetheless the importance of our conflict model lies in this, that it does not exclude change because of the nature of its concepts. It is implicit in the way in which the facts are conceptualized, when such a model is applied to them, that change is expected to take place. This is precisely what the model of an organism or an equilibrium excludes. Thus we have a way of formulating sociological theory which not only explains structure and process within a closed system, but which also explains the changes which occur from one system to another.

In the next chapter we shall consider some of the problems which arise in applying our model to the problems of the theory of social class as that term is usually understood. When we have

134

done this we shall return to the problems of scientific method which arise in applying the model to empirical research.

VIII

CONFLICT AND THE
ANALYSIS OF CLASS

CLASS AND STATUS

IN the last chapter it was inevitable that we should become concerned with the problem of social classes. For in one of its usages the term 'class' has been defined very largely in terms of conflict situations of a disruptive type. But it will be instructive now to approach the problem from the other side, starting with the problems which have arisen in the actual empirical study of class, in order to see how far these problems are understandable in terms of the theoretical models we have been discussing.

The most striking fact about studies of 'social class' in contemporary sociology has been the confusion of two analytically distinct conceptions, on the one hand the concept of class as used by Marx, and on the other the concept used by Lloyd Warner and others to refer to hierarchical status groupings in small communities. So, for instance, one sometimes hears sociologists speaking of Warner refuting Marx, and, on the other hand, Marxists have often tended to regard acceptance of Warner's conclusions as a central sociological heresy. By contrast, for some at least of the great European sociologists, there was no question of these two concepts being confused. Weber and Tönnies, especially, distinguished clearly between them, and any theoretical approach to the problem of class can do no better than to go back to the distinctions which they draw.[1]

It must be pointed out at once, however, that the two concepts

[1] *See* Bendix and Lipset, *Class, Status and Power* (1954), pp. 49–74.

are only analytically distinct. This can be seen in two ways. On the one hand when we consider what those whom we observe, the actors in the social system, mean by class, it becomes obvious that they do not distinguish between the two conceptions. For them the word class is used to describe complex situations involving both economic classes and status classes. On the other hand when the two analytic conceptions are developed further it becomes clear that the particular line of development of an economic-class situation is bound to be affected by the sort of status situation which exists within the social system as a whole and vice versa. What we have to do now is to look at the models implied by each of these concepts in turn and seek to understand the way in which class and status systems intersect in actual social situations.

THE CONCEPT OF CLASS AS A CONFLICT GROUP

What Marx's model of class-conflict suggests is a particular sub-type of the conflict situation which we have discussed. His particular area of interest is in those basic conflict situations which arise because of the differential relations which various sets of actors have to the means of production. The essence of his 'materialism' (which is not a necessary implication of anything which has been said in the previous chapter) lies in his assertion that this sub-type is the crucial form of conflict around which the social system must develop in any society. Moreover Marx is interested in the special case in which the social relations of production produces a labour-market in which the owners of the means of production buy the labour of the non-owners.

Weber's conception of economic classes is somewhat wider in scope. It includes not merely those cases in which conflict and bargaining arise from differential relations to the means of production, but all cases in which there is a market situation. Thus he says,

> In our terminology 'classes' are not communities; they merely represent possible and frequent bases for communal action. We may speak of class when (1) a number of people have in common a specific casual component of their life chances insofar as (2) this component is represented exclusively by economic interest in the possession of goods and opportunities for income and (3) is represented under the conditions of the commodity or labour markets.

[These points refer to 'class situation' which we may express more briefly as the typical chance for a supply of goods, external living conditions, and personal life experiences, insofar as this chance is determined by the kind and the amount of power, or lack of such, to dispose of goods or skills for income in a given economic order. The term class refers to any group of people that is found in the same class situation].[1]

Weber then goes on to specify some of the important bases of class formation in human history.

'Property' and 'lack of property' are the basic categories of all class situations . . .
Within these categories, however, class situations are further differentiated: on the one hand, according to the kind of property which is useable for returns: and, on the other hand, according to the kind of services that can be offered on the market. Ownership of domestic buildings; productive establishments; warehouses, stores, agriculturally useable land; large and small holdings—quantitative differences with possible qualitative consequences—; ownership of mines, cattle; men (slaves); disposition over mobile instruments of production, or capital goods of all sorts, especially money or objects that can be exchanged for money easily and at any time; disposition over products of one's own labour or of other's labour differing according to their various distances from consumability; disposition over transferable monopolies of any kind—all these distinctions differentiate the class situations of the propertied, just as does the meaning that they can and do give to the utilization of their property, especially to property which has monetary equivalence.[2]

There are three points at which Weber's definitions of 'class' and 'class situation' differentiate his approach from that of Marx. These are:— (1) that he includes situations other than those arising from differential relationship to the means of production (e.g. ownership of domestic buildings) (2) that in the case of the latter he recognizes a greater variety of relationships to the means of production (e.g. he says that they may be differentiated according to the kind of services offered, and later distinguishes between small and large landownership. For Marx landowners and wage-earners constitute single groups); and (3) that people's class situations differ according to 'the meaning that they can and do give to the utilization of their property'.

[1] Bendix and Lipset, *Op. cit.*, p. 64. [2] *Ibid.*, p. 65.

The second and third of these points are of most importance in relation to the argument of the present chapter. The second raises the question 'Why should there be differences in the "life-chances" of the different sub-groups amongst those who own and those who do not own the means of production?' The third leads us to ask what Weber means by 'the meaning that they give to the utilization of their property'. We shall have to consider what the relationship is between this meaning and what we have variously called the aims, aspirations and interests of groups.

These questions are of considerable importance in the analysis of the class structure of contemporary societies. One central question for example in the sociology of class to-day is whether the so-called middle-classes are really to be regarded as a class. Do they really have different 'life-chances' or is their belief that they do merely a case of 'false consciousness'? Here the second point leads naturally to a consideration of the third, for the possibility of the middle-classes becoming separated from the proletariat seems to depend in part at least on the 'meaning' which they give to their situation. The Marxist notion of 'false consciousness' has often led to the view that the difference between a middle-class and a proletarian class situation is 'merely' a subjective one, and therefore not important because a valid theory of class should be based on 'objective' factors.

Marx himself was by no means unaware of these problems even though he failed to treat them at any length. He was approaching a statement of the central questions in the last few pages of Volume III of *Capital*, when he writes,

What constitutes wage-labourers, capitalists and landlords as three great classes?
At first glance it might seem that the identity of revenues and of sources of revenue is responsible. The classes are three great social groups whose components, the individual members, live from wages, profit and rent respectively, that is from the utilization of their labour power, capital and landed property.
However from this point of view doctors and officials would also form distinct classes. for they belong to different social groups and the revenue of the members of each group come from the same source. The same would be true of the infinite distinction of interest

139

and position which the social division of labour creates among workers, as among capitalists and landowners.[1]

It is clear that Marx does not believe that true class differentiation proceeds as far as this. Although the bases of class-formation appear to be there, classes, as such, do not emerge. Indeed, even in the case of the working-class, class formation is by no means the automatic consequence of position in relation to the means of production or in the labour market. Thus differences in the relationship of groups to the means of production may be a necessary, but it is not a sufficient condition for class formation.

According to Marx the final factor necessary for the emergence of a true class is its participation in a 'political struggle'. Thus he makes a distinction in Hegelian terms between a 'class-in-itself' and a 'class-for-itself'. The former term refers to a group with a common class-situation only, and the latter to a group which is organized for conflict. He makes the point in *The Poverty of Philosophy* when he says,

> Economic conditions had in the first place transformed the mass of the people into workers. The domination of capital created the common situation and common interests of this class. Thus the mass is already a class in relation to capital, but not yet a class-for-itself. In the struggle, of which we have only indicated a few phases, this mass unites and forms itself into a class-for-itself. The interests which it defends become class interests. But the struggle between classes is a political struggle.[2]

This passage is readily understandable in terms of the discussion of the last chapter. There we saw in trying to construct an adequate model of conflict-group formation that the category of the ends of group action had to be understood in two stages. First there was the fact of a number of separate individuals finding themselves in similar conflict situations and thus developing like interests. But this resulted in the formation of a group whose object was not directly the pursuit of these interests, but rather the mobilization of power to strengthen the numbers of the group in their 'struggle' or bargaining. The sociological explanation of the behaviour of the members was

[1] Marx, *Capital* (1909), Vol. III, pp. 1031–1032. *See* Coser and Rosenberg, *Sociological Theory*, p. 369.

[2] Marx, *The Poverty of Philosophy* (1910). *See* Bottomore and Rubel, *Karl Marx, Selected Sociological Writings* (1956), p. 187.

then seen to lie in relating this behaviour not to the like-interests of the members, but to the group's aims or interests. There is no great difference between this position and that outlined by Marx in the above passage, except that we should prefer for the sake of clarity to speak of like rather than common interests before the group was formed.

But there is an extremely important point here and one which will help us to see the relationship between Marx's theory and theories such as that of Weber. The determining factor for Marx is not that of the original like interests of the class-members. It is the situation of 'political struggle'. Is there not a link here between this feature of Marx's theory and Weber's distinction between 'property' and 'lack of property' as the basic categories of all class situations and differentiations according to the meaning which people in a common class situation give to the utilization of their property.

Marxists, on the whole, are very suspicious of any attempt to extend Marx's meaning here. They would distinguish between the real aims of the class in a situation of political struggle and purely ideological aims which represent a false consciousness. In particular they would insist that the 'middle-classes' do not have really different class aims to those of the proletariat, however many false meanings they might give to their situation.

Now one factor in Marxist theory which pushes it towards this position is that it tends towards a type of positivism, in the sense in which that term was used in Chapter Six. It is inherently suspicious of the introduction of normative factors into its theory of action. This is one of the implications of Marx's 'materialism'. In reacting against Hegelian idealism and 'standing the dialectic on its head', he was bound to emphasise precisely the factors which idealism neglects, factors such as material needs and interests.

Yet Marx was no crude materialist as is shown by his first thesis on Feuerbach and by the quotation which we have made from *The Poverty of Philosophy*. He does recognize that new aims are introduced into a situation when individuals not only pursue their like interests but also engage in 'political struggle'. It would therefore be entirely consistent with Marxist theory for us to look very closely at the possible class situations and at the development of class aims in the course of political struggle.

The crucial case here is that of the so-called middle-class. There do appears to be good reasons for suggesting that its class-situation differs from that of the proletariat, at least in the case of some middle class groups. This is particularly true with regard to managerial groups.

Weber has sometimes been accused of being blind to the fact of the class struggle in his analysis of capitalist social structure. To some extent, perhaps, this is true. But it is sometimes overlooked that in his study of bureaucracies he made a peculiarly penetrating analysis of the relationship between one large group of roles and the means of production. This analysis is highly relevant to the question of whether the middle-classes are really a separate class.

One surprising feature of this analysis, when one looks at it in detail, is the number of similarities between the situation of the bureaucrat, as he describes it, and the situation of the proletariat as it is described by Marx. Like the proletarian the bureaucrat has no property rights in the facilities which are essential for his work. Like the proletarian he is dependent upon his remuneration for his livelihood. And like the proletarian his working-life and interests have to be completely separated from his home. Where then lies the difference?

The crucial differentiating fact is that the bureaucrat believes that he has a career for life whereas the proletarian may be discharged at very short notice. To put this in epigrammatic form we may say that the proletarian sells his labour by the week, whereas the bureaucrat sells it by the life. The question, however, is whether this distinction is a valid one. Is the bureaucrat under an illusion here which may be shattered at any time by a letter from his superior officer telling him that his services are no longer required? If he is, then his apparent class-position may indeed be merely a product of false consciousness which he may expect to be swept away as the 'real' factors of the situation become operative.

What we should say, using the terminology of earlier chapters, is that his 'expectations' are relevant to the description of his class-position. The social structure may be defined in terms of these expectations in either of two sets of circumstances. Either they are valid expectations in the sense that 'alter' (in this case, his employer) recognizes them as binding, or they are valid in the sense that he can force his employer to accept them. So far as higher level bureaucrats are concerned the first alternative holds. So far as lower level bureaucrats, and indeed some workers, are concerned the second might be the case, although the instances of trade-unions successfully winning more than a few additional weeks' notice for their members are few and far between.

The point to notice, however, is that when a group of individuals has *valid* expectations about its situation these expectations cannot be discussed as merely subjective. There appears to be good reason for holding, therefore, that there is a considerable number of managers and bureaucrats in any advanced industrial society, who, although they would appear only as deluded proletarians according to rigid Marxist definitions, do actually have a distinct class situation. Similarly it could be shown that the specialist workers of modern industry whose knowledge is both scarce and indispensible enjoy a greater measure of security than, and have a different class situation from the proletariat.

This does not necessarily mean that the middle-class will become a separate class-for-itself in Marx's sense. By definition they would only do so if they became caught up in a 'political struggle' or as we should say in a conflict situation. Insofar, however, as their expectations of a career or of permanent security are fulfilled they face no such conflict, at least with their employers. For them the social arrangements which their employers suggest are entirely legitimate. For such people the only way in which they are likely to become involved in a class struggle is on the side of their employers, the aims of whose social system they accept as binding on themselves.

Of course this does not exclude the emergence of middle-class conflict groups in other contexts. One factor which may be important is one to which Weber refers in his list of factors producing different class-situations, namely, 'the ownership of domestic buildings'. Certainly the distinction between those who pay rent, those to whom it is paid, and those who own their own houses either outright or through mortgages, is an important factor in local politics. But this is to widen the basis of the discussion.

More important to our consideration of Marxist theory is the fact that there are many lower-level bureaucrats, skilled workers and clerks whose situation appears marginal between that of the proletarian and the contented middle-class. Such groups, as Lockwood has shown in his perceptive study of clerical workers,[1] are in a continual dilemma. Should they rely upon the paternalistic benevolence of their employers, or should they put their faith in trades unions? This dilemma is of crucial importance to the theory of class.

It is at this point that our observations in the previous chapter become relevant. There we saw that in a ruling class situation the ruling class would be continually trying to ensure its own position by trying to convince members of other classes that its position was 'legitimate'. Equally the leaders of the subject class will seek to deny this claim to legitimacy. Naturally, then, their appeal will be directed to the marginal groups which we are discussing, and the actual position of these groups in the social structure will depend upon which interpretation of their situation they accept.

This would appear to involve a fairly considerable revision of the Marxist model of class conflict as it is normally understood. Yet it is one which must be accepted unless it is possible to argue with Marx that the economic development of capitalism *must* involve 'the increasing misery' of the proletariat. But until this increasing misery is actually experienced it is irrelevant to the problem of class formation.

THE CONCEPT OF STATUS

So far we have focused our attention fairly narrowly on conflicts arising out of economic or market situations, on the assumption that such conflicts are of strategic importance in the structure of modern societies. Even in this sphere we have found that the notion of 'legitimacy' and of its denial is important to the understanding of the way in which conflicts develop. We must now turn to a sphere in which this notion is even more important, namely, that of status systems. We shall suggest that such systems can only be adequately understood in terms of claims to legitimate authority and their rejection by some members of society.

Once again it is as well to begin with Weber's definition of a status situation which is as follows:— 'In contrast to the purely economically determined "class situation" we wish to designate

[1] Lockwood, *The Blackcoated Worker* (1958).

as "status situation" every typical component of the life of men that is determined by a specific, positive or negative, social estimation of honour. This honour may be connected with any quality shared by a plurality.'[1]

Now it would seem at first sight that the differential apportionment of honour or esteem would be an obvious feature of any society or grouping, and this need have no necessary relation to a system of economic classes. One would expect that winning such esteem would be one of the rewards or sanctions which would encourage the performance of roles and so reinforce the social structure. But the generalized conception of a status system implies something more than and something different from this. It implies not merely the apportionment of esteem for some specific role performance but the apportionment of a generalized esteem which serves to segregate one group from another and to facilitate the development of different ways of life.

The questions which are raised therefore by the existence of status systems are three. (1) What are the characteristics whose possession leads to the possessor enjoying high or low esteem? (2) How is the tendency to assign esteem in this way to be explained? and (3) Who accords the esteem?

Different qualities will, if they are chosen as the criteria for the assignment of esteem, produce systems of different types. Thus, ancestry, which forms a component element of status evaluations in most systems, naturally tends to produce a closed system with little social mobility, best exemplified by the case of the Indian caste system. If the possession of money is the crucial factor, a greater measure of mobility may be possible, and if education is decisive, there may be, provided that there is equality of educational opportunity, the highest degree of mobility of all.

But one important factor regarding the differential distribution of esteem according to the possession of valued characteristics should not be overlooked. This is that very often it is not the possession of the crucial qualities themselves which are important, but the symbols of their possession. Thus what seems to matter in most status systems is not so much the possession of a quality such as those mentioned above which matters as the living of a certain 'style of life'. Partly this style

---

[1] Bendix and Lipset, *Op. cit.*, p. 68.

of life is merely the consequence of the social isolation brought about by the status system. Partly it is the consequence of attempts by the incumbents of high status, albeit unconscious, to restrict entry to their group.

The fact that, once status groupings exist, differences between them tend to multiply seems to make it difficult in most cases to say what the determining factor is. There is, for example, the well-known problem of the down-at-heel aristocrat. Originally, may be, the high esteem which his ancestor enjoyed depended upon his role as a landed proprietor fulfilling an important social function. But his ancestors developed a style of life which he retains even though he has been stripped of his functions, and it is this style of life which leads him to enjoy a higher degree of esteem than people who have taken over his functions.

Thus the question 'what are the determining characteristics of a status group?' appears to yield no clear answer. And it is a question which had led to much fruitless and confusing debate especially when what has been sought has been thought to be not the criterion of status assignment, but, more generally, of something called 'class'. All that we can say is that many societies are characterized by the existence of communal groupings each with its own way of life, which are thought by the population to be hierarchically arranged in some order of esteem.

But this leads us to the second question of why esteem is assigned to ways of life in this way. Few sociologists have been prepared to accept that it is quite arbitrarily assigned, but it would seem that the explanation most often put forward is a peculiarly implausible one. It is a version of the general functionalist theory, which has been applied to the analysis of status systems by Davis and Moore. As they put it,

> If the rights and perquisites of different positions in a society must be unequal, then the society must be stratified, because that is what stratifications means. Social inequality is thus an unconsciously evolved device by which societies insure that the most important positions are conscientiously filled by the most qualified persons. Hence every society, no matter how simple or complex, must differentiate persons both in terms of prestige and esteem and must therefore possess a certain amount of institutionalized inequality.[1]

[1] Davis and Moore, 'Some principles of Stratification', in Coser and Rosenberg, *Op. cit.*, pp. 408–419.

146

But how far is it true that the 'most important positions' are those which receive the greatest esteem? What standard of importance is to be applied? From whose point of view are the positions most important? Prima facie it does not seem to be the case that positions of the greatest *utilitarian* importance receive the greatest esteem. On the contrary the usual case seems to be that in which the most esteemed positions are those of symbolic or even only decorative character. Of course it could be argued that they must be the most important, despite appearances, *because* they enjoy high esteem. But this is to beg the question. One is reminded of Malinowski arguing that the survival of the hansom cab is to be explained functionally by the fact that it ministers to our 'retrospective sentiments'. Once it is assumed that everything has a function, a function must be found or invented for everything. Similarly once it is assumed that the positions of greatest importance enjoy the greatest esteem some account of the importance of positions enjoying great esteem will be put forward.

In fact the only variant of the functionalist view which in any way seems plausible is that which holds that esteem is accorded to those positions which were *historically* of importance. This would certainly be a more convincing explanation of such facts as the high esteem enjoyed by the British aristocracy or the old families of Warner's Yankee city. Even here, however, there are two important objections which may be made. The first is that in these cases the prestige of the positions might simply derive from their age rather than their importance. The other is that such groups do not enjoy universal esteem. They are very often derided or resented by the other status-groups.

This brings us to the third and more important question, namely, 'When it is said that esteem is accorded to positions of greater importance, by whom is it accorded?' The answer which is often assumed here appears to be 'It is accorded by common consent', and one can in theory imagine a state of affairs in which everyone did agree on what characteristics and what style of life merited esteem. But once again this pure type appears to have little relevance to our actual experience of status systems. It is an obvious fact of our experience that where birth is claimed as a criterion of status it is challenged by those who would wish to replace it by money, education, occupation or social function. And each of these would be challenged by all the others. Even occupation, which, it had been thought for some time, provided an agreed criterion, gives rise to conflicting valuations. This has been clearly shown in a recent article by Turner.[1] Turner showed that where people were asked to place occupations in terms of merited prestige rather than in terms of status rank-order (the question here always involved asking people what they thought other people thought), different occupational groups as respondents showed considerable conflict in their evaluation of the different occupations.

Clearly the best that can be said is that the case in which there is unanimity on status valuations is a limiting one rarely, if ever, found empirically. The usual case is that in which there is considerable conflict as to what the criterion of status should be. In a sense one might say that each of the groups was proposing its own alternative criteria and fighting to get them universally accepted. Thus it would be true to say that a conflict of status-ideologies is an essential part of all status-class relations. This ideological conflict, however, might be of an even more fundamental kind, because what some groups propose is not merely a different criterion for status assignment, but the rejection of the very notion of status itself.

LLOYD WARNER'S ACCOUNT OF THE YANKEE CITY STATUS SYSTEM

Indeed what are described by the students of status-hierarchies look very little like the pure type of status groups which we have been considering. It will be useful, therefore, to look a little more closely at one outstanding study in this field, that of Lloyd Warner and his associates,[2] and ask whether there is not some more adequate theoretical model available to explain the facts which he describes. What we shall suggest is that (1) the notion of a status hierarchy is something which is deeply entrenched in the ideology of the ruling classes (in the sense of conflict classes) as a means of gaining recognition for the legitimacy of their position; (2) this ruling class will attempt to get the status ideology accepted by other classes and (3) that these other classes do not all accept it, but put forward counter ideologies of their own. To explain this we must refer to Warner's

[1] Turner, 'Life Situation and Sub-culture'. *British Journal of Sociology*, Vol. IX, No. 4. December 1958, p. 299.
[2] Warner and Lunt, *The Social System of a Modern Community*.

account of the behaviour of his six classes in Yankee City. The following is a summary of some of the more important things which he says about them.

1. *The Upper-Upper (U.U.) Class*. The members of this class have wealth inherited through several generations. The original source of this wealth is not shoe manufacture, the currently most productive source, but ship-building which was the most important source in its day. The U.U. class has its own neighbourhoods, cliques and associations, as well as participating in associations through which it can exercise authority over other classes.

2. *The Lower-Upper (L.U.) Class*. The members of this class consist of the factory owners and their friends. They are the new rich and their behaviour is characterized by conspicuous consumption. They have their own neighbourhoods, cliques and associations as well as associations through which they exercise influence downwards, but above all they seek closer association with the U.U. class and seek to convert their wealth into the outward symbolism of U.U. status. As a defence against this intrusion, the U.U. group makes ever more exquisite distinctions of behaviour through which it seeks to preserve its own identity.

3. *The Upper-Middle (U.M.) Class*. This class consists of substantial business men, managers and professional people. They spend much less time in conspicuous consumption and play a leading part in civic activities.

4. *The Lower-Middle (L.M.) Class*. This class consists of small-scale business men, white-collar groups and some skilled workers. They are not very wealthy but place great emphasis upon the virtues of cleanliness, sobriety and respectability. It is in this class that the notion of 'keeping up with the Jones's' is most applicable.

5. *The Upper-Lower (U.L.) Class*. This class consists of the bulk of the manual workers, or as one of Warner's informants calls them 'the clean poor'. They tend to belong to trade unions, lodges and friendly societies, and to reject the notion of paternalistic management in favour of trade unionism and collective bargaining. They feel a special contempt for the behaviour of the L.U. class.

149

6. *The Lower-Lower (L.L.) Class.* This group consists of the demoralized poor, who are very often unemployed and dependent for their livelihood on social security payments. They are resentful and contemptuous of all other classes and philosophies about the superiority of their own relatively undisciplined way of life.

THE REAL SIGNIFICANCE OF LLOYD WARNER'S CLASSES
THE L.U'S CLAIM TO LEGITIMACY

Now whatever else may be said it is clear that there is no consensus of status valuations here. At every point, even at the point of contact between U.U. and L.U. there is conflict about who is entitled to the greatest esteem and who should be allowed to move from group to group.

For a deeper understanding of this system it is necessary to begin by looking at the motivation and behaviour of the L.U. class, which is crucial to the system as a whole. They clearly do accept the idea of some sort of status order and spend their lives attempting to break into the one class which they recognize as being higher in the hierarchy than their own. Why do they do this and what do they gain by it?

The behaviour of the L.U. class is readily explained if we look at the *economic* position in which they find themselves. They find themselves, because of their position as factory owners, in a position of supreme power in the community. But they do not have legitimate authority. The lower order continually compare them unfavourably with the ruling classes of the past. Hence they must, if they are to gain acceptance, abolish the distinctions between themselves and this class. At the same time they need the U.U. class and its way of life, because without it there would be no way at all of legitimating their positions. On the other hand they have to keep the lower orders in their place and the idea of an overall status hierarchy, rationalized on the lines suggested by Davis and Moore, provides them with the necessary ideology. Thus the idea of a status system is not something which emerges, as it were, from the general will. It is an L.U. idea, which fits in well with the L.U.'s need to maintain its own power.

The U.U. class has its own reasons for approving of the system which the L.U.'s seek to introduce. It should not be thought that the esteem which this class currently enjoys is something which has existed from time immemorial. They were 'new rich' in their day, and it was only when they were replaced by even less charming successors that they began to win popular approval. Now, however, they find the working-classes and the new new-rich conspiring to elevate their status. Naturally they will do everything they can to encourage them. They may resent the L.U's trying to gate-crash their tea-parties, but without the situation which the L.U.'s have produced, the tea-parties would have little excitement.

The U.M. class also has reasons of its own for accepting the status hierarchy. Their ambitions are limited in any case, but they can achieve them far more readily in the setting which the L.U.'s have created. They have a delegated authority and not inconsiderable perquisites to reward them for accepting the system. Moreover, in the immediate context of community life they do win approval for their social usefulness.

The behaviour of the L.M. and L.L. classes are both best understood in terms of Merton's analysis of *Social Structure and Anomie*.[1] According to this analysis the American ethos makes impossible demands on the majority of the population and there are various ways of adapting to them without full compliance. In this case the characteristic behaviour of the L.M. and L.L. classes can be understood as an adaptation to the impossible demands made by the status systems.

The impossibility of the demands of the American ethos, according to Merton, derives from the fact that it not only insists that successful goal achievement is necessary, but that it also insists that certain means and these means only may be used in the process. Not all can fulfil these demands and hence there are groups which give up the goal of success, groups which introduce illegitimate means, and groups which abandon both the goal and the means. The two forms of adaptation which are relevant here are the first and the third, which Merton calls Ritualism and Retreatism.

The Ritualist says 'I may not have got to the top, but at least I have stuck to the rules', and implies 'Not like some people I could name!' He will not 'stick his neck out', but likes to be able to point to the rule-book to prove that he has played fair. These are exactly the characteristics of L.M. behaviour.

[1] Merton, *Social Theory and Social Structure*, Chapter IV.

L

'Keeping up with the Jones's' does not imply getting ahead of the Jones's. Such an ambition has been given up long ago. The L.M. class is not motivated for out-and-out status striving. All it wants is to be able to prove its respectability.

By contrast with the ritualists who say 'I am poor, but I was honest', the retreatists say 'I may be poor and unsuccessful, but I am free'. Here we find our L.L. philosophers with their contempt for the goals, the ways of life, and the institutionalized means of the status-mad world. Their reaction to the proposal for regarding the world as a status-hierarchy is to retreat from it altogether.

But what of the class which we have left out, the U.L.'s? What is their attitude to the idea of a status hierarchy? It is surely that they, too, have rejected the idea of status-striving, but that they have put in its place a demand for security and respect, where they are, and as of right. Parsons sees this when he says,

> In the lower reaches of the structure there are tendencies to deviation from the middle-class pattern . . . Essentially we might say that this consists in a shift from the predominance of the success goal to that of the security goal. More concretely it is a loss of interest in achievement, whether for its own sake and for the opportunity to do more important things, or for the advancement of family status through more income or increased reputation. Occupational role then becomes not the main field for achievement, but a means of securing the necessities of a tolerable standard of living, a necessary evil.[1]

Taken, all in all, it seems that in the case of the three lower classes at least, status-striving in its pure form does not exist. The picture of Yankee City which Warner draws is not one which can be comprehended in terms of the pure type of status model. Is there a model which can explain it?

In fact it seems that the sort of situation which Warner describes is one which is readily explained in terms of the conflict model outlined in our previous chapter if it is spelled out in more detail to take account of the notions of class and status which we have discussed here.

The basic fact is that this is a case of the ruling-class situation which is one of the possibilities arising out of social conflict.

[1] Parsons, 'Revised Analytic Approach to the Theory of Social Stratification', in Bendix and Lipset, *Op. cit.*, p. 125.

In this case the L.U. class is the ruling class. One would expect such a class, in terms of our model to seek some means of legitimating its position. In this case the means which it uses is that of offering an interpretation of the existing distribution of power and privileges in terms of a status system.

The notion of a status system is one which is fairly readily acceptable, because, in any group with a specific purpose, our experience as participants is that we do esteem most highly those people who fulfil roles which are manifestly useful in relation to the group's purpose. What the status ideology does is to extend this notion in two directions. On the one hand it applies it not to a group with a specific purpose, but to a total community and, on the other, it applies it to a situation in which there is a ruling class whose interests may conflict with those of the classes whom they rule, and whose position rests in the first place on the power, rather than the authority, which they exercise.

As we pointed out in our previous chapter, however, the ruling class is not always successful in getting its interpretations of society and its claim to legitimacy accepted. Counter-ideologies which deny this claim tend to be put forward by the leaders of the lower classes. The main case on which we dwelt in our original analysis was that in which the ideology was one which pointed a conflict of interests and emphasized the balance of power element in the inter-class situations. This would explain the typical attitudes and behaviour of Warner's U.L. class. The behaviour of the L.M. and L.L. classes suggests other ways in which a class may interpret its behaviour, once it denies the legitimacy of the order proposed by its rulers. Both involve forms of accommodation to the system of power prevailing without involving positive motivation to accept it in its entirety.

THE ANALYSIS OF CLASS CONFLICT IN RELATION TO GENERAL SOCIOLOGY

Now what we have shown in this chapter is of some importance in relation to the whole question of the general approach which sociologists should make to research problems. The empiricist approaches the subject of class with a demand for a simple clear operational definition of the phenomena to be studied. In

Durkheim's words he wants to be told 'the empirical character-istics of the thing designated'. Thus class is defined either in terms of some simple objective characteristic such as income, education, etc., or in the case of the more sophisticated empiri-cists in terms of the subjective attitudes of people towards class. Thereafter they feel that enough has been done to define class and go on to discuss such problems as the extent of mobility from one class to another.

What we have shown here is that in two separate areas of study, one the study of economic classes and the other the study of status classes, their definitions are inadequate and misleading. In the first case we saw that the notion of classes being formed on the basis of the relation of individuals and groups to the means of production was much more complex and allowed for a far greater variety of classes than the cruder forms of Marxism would lead us to expect. In the second case we found that the actual attitudes operative amongst people thought to be living in a hierarchial status system involved great tensions and conflict within that system. Nonetheless, the groupings which are formed as a result of the interests and attitudes which we have discussed are explicable in terms of a single general theory of conflict. If we understood this theory better we should approach research into social class with much more adequate though complex definitions of what the classes are, and we should not be in danger of producing studies which, although statistically exact, were irrelevant to the problem of class structure.

It should not be thought that this is meant as a criticism of mobility studies as such. Far from this being the case, once we had a picture of the conflict, power, and status relations holding between the classes, any changes in the extent of mobility would be very relevant evidence as to the nature of the class system. Obviously it matters greatly to a system if parents expect their children to move into a different class, and if the existing members of a class are continually having to accept new recruits from other classes to membership. But it also matters that this transition process involves taking over or failing to take over complex patterns of motivation appropriate to the new class situation.

It is also of prime importance in predicting the behaviour of social classes to understand the complexity of their members' motivation. Someone has recently said half-humourously that the British working class not merely believes in the class struggle, but in the necessity of its everlasting continuance. This is just one of many class attitudes which is readily explained in terms of the sort of conflict model advocated in this book. The problem is a far more complicated one than can be dealt with by a simple reference to the statistics of occupational distribution. In fact studies of this kind usually make large tacit assumptions about the relations between classes, which if they were made explicit would not stand up to examination.

In fact what this chapter shows very clearly is that in this, one of the central questions studied in empirical sociology, there is a complex interrelationship between variable elements and that, hence, the problems in the field can only really be stated by someone with an adequate theoretical orientation to the subject. This, of course, has been a major theme of the argument throughout this book.

But this leads on to our final problem. Empiricist sociology has the undoubted advantage that, though irrelevant and lacking in significance, its conclusions are readily verifiable. Our problem is to show whether the complex theoretical models which we have been elaborating can be subjected to any empirical test. Theory is important and indeed essential to science. But without the possibility of empirical verification it remains sheer speculation. We must now ask the question 'How "scientific" can sociology be?'

IX

OBJECTIVITY AND PROOF
IN SOCIOLOGY

M AX WEBER held that the sociologist was required to give 'explanations which were adequate on the level of meaning' and also 'causally adequate' explanations.[1] In this chapter we shall be concerned to discover what could be meant by these two sorts of explanation and in so doing we shall see how far it is possible for sociology to employ the complex theoretical constructs suggested here and yet at the same time live up to the requirements of empirical science.

WEBER'S CONCEPTION OF 'UNDERSTANDING'

Weber himself had to deal with a tradition in which it was held that the two sorts of explanation mentioned are incompatible with one another, and it will help us to see what he meant by them if we consider the way in which he dealt with the arguments of his predecessors. In particular it is necessary to begin by considering the approach to the social sciences expounded by Wilhelm Dilthey.[2]

Dilthey's approach is in the idealist tradition and he might be said to hold an idealist theory of action and culture in the precise sense in which Parsons uses the term. In such a theory, to quote Parsons again:— 'Spatiotemporal phenomena become related

[1] Weber, *Theory of Social and Economic Organization*, Chapter 1.
[2] *See* Hodges, *Wilhelm Dilthey, An Introduction* (1949), and *The Philosophy of Wilhelm Dilthey* (1952).

to action only as symbolic "modes of expression" or "embodiments" of "meaning".[1] The task of the sociologist then is, for Dilthey, one of seeking to 'understand' these meanings.

The techniques necessary for such understanding, however, are quite distinct from those of science. The best way of describing them is to point to the analogy of someone learning a foreign language by going to live amongst a people who speak it. At first he understands nothing, but gradually the relation between things and situations on the one hand and the verbal symbols which they evoke becomes clear. Eventually one discovers that one has learnt the language and the meaning of people's speech becomes understandable. Similarly in dealing with a strange culture or a period of history the sociologist has gradually to piece together some sort of total picture of the meaning of action and culture. It is this process which is called 'understanding'.

The techniques of understanding in Dilthey's sense cannot be set out more clearly than this. At one place he describes them as a form of 'self-surrender' which 'makes the inner being of the time-born historian into a universe which mirrors the whole historical world'.[2] He suggests that the skills needed by a historian are more akin to those of the poet than a scientist and claims that the greatest history has always been written in the great ages of poetry.

The scientific method Dilthey identifies with the search for general laws and these he claims are of no importance in the social sciences. Thus he writes:— 'The uniformities which can be established in the field of society are in numbers, importance and precision far behind the laws which it has been possible to lay down for nature on the same foundation of relations in space and time.'[3]

Against this Weber adopts two positions both of which are of importance to our argument. The first is that there is a form of understanding which can be set out in a manner not incompatible with the methods of science, and the second that social science does not necessarily depend upon generalization or abstract systems of laws.

The key to his first point is his emphasis upon the rational

---

[1] Parsons, *The Structure of Social Action*, p. 82.
[2] Wilhelm Dilthey, *An Introduction*, p. 137.
[3] *Ibid.*, p. 145.

type of action. Here we do not need to 'know the language' because if the action is rational the actor will use the scientifically appropriate means and what these are can be known to anyone who has access to the conclusions of empirical science. Hence it is perfectly possible to see the process of understanding in this case as one in which we put forward a hypothesis which explains any action by referring it to an end which the actor is thought of as pursuing by rational means. Provided we admit that it is legitimate to formulate such hypotheses in subjective terms, there is no difficulty about this.

Weber's own arguments rests heavily upon the understanding of rational actions of this kind and he explicitly argues that one should first seek to explain action in such rational terms and then go on to formulate further explanations to explain deviations. This is quite legitimate and would take us much further in explaining a culture pattern than Dilthey with his idealistic bias would lead us to suppose.

But there is a further argument about the explanations of the non-rational types of action. Dilthey's argument was that the relation between a symbol and the thing symbolized was always arbitary, and the same argument applies to the ritual rules which we suggested played the same role in non-rational action as the laws of empirical science did in the rational case. However one can hold all this without also holding that it is impossible to make explicit the hypotheses in terms of which one explains non-rational action. The difficulty is not that theoretical hypotheses cannot be found. It is simply that we are working far more in the dark than we are when we are dealing with rational action. But the difficulties are no greater here than they are in natural science. In trying to explain rational action we are especially fortunate in that our own experience is similar to that of the actors whom we study and we can draw on this experience as a short cut in finding hypotheses. But when we are denied this short cut we are merely in the ordinary position of an empirical scientist in the natural sciences. We can still put forward a hypothesis which states the hypothetical actor's end and the 'ritual rules' which govern his choice of means.

The second point made by Weber is that concerning the role of generalization in sociology. Here he takes his stand with some of his German predecessors, particularly Rickert, against positivism. It does seem that Weber's position altered during his lifetime because by the time he came to write *Wirtschaft und Gesellschaft*[1] he had apparently come to accept the necessity of some sort of generalized theoretical laws, albeit of a formal kind. However he never explicitly disavowed the methodological positions taken up in his original essay on objectivity[2] and it is the viewpoint expounded in that essay which is of relevance here.

Weber argues that all science is faced with a problem of selecting from the infinitude of data which is presented to it. But whereas in natural science the principle of selection is that it is the recurrent phenomena which are worthy of study, in the social sciences the principle must be that of 'relevance for value', that is to say that we should study those phenomena which are connected with the attainment of certain 'values' with which we are concerned.

As Weber puts it:—

> The significance of a configuration of cultural phenomena and the basis of this significance cannot however be derived and rendered intelligible by a system of analytic laws, however perfect it may be, since the significance of cultural events presupposes a value-orientation towards these events. The concept of culture is a value-concept. Empirical reality becomes 'culture' to us because and in so far as we relate it to value ideas. It includes those segments and only those segments of reality which have become significant to us because of their value-relevance. Only a small portion of existing concrete reality is coloured by our value-conditioned interest and it alone is significant to us. It is significant because it reveals relationships which are important to us due to their connection with our values. Only because and to the extent that this is the case is it worthwhile for us to know its individual features. We cannot discover, however, what is meaningful to us by a 'presuppositionless' investigation of empirical data. Rather perception of its meaningfulness to us is the presupposition of its becoming an object of investigation. Meaningfulness naturally does not coincide with laws as such, and the more general the law the less the coincidence.[3]

Weber reached this position as the result of his participation in a debate about the nature of the cultural studies conducted

---

[1] Four chapters of which are translated in *The Theory of Social and Economic Organization*.
[2] In *The Methodology of the Social Sciences*, pp. 50–112.
[3] *Ibid.*, p. 76–77.

with the neo-Kantians and Dilthey. But it should be noticed that our discussion of the action frame of reference and functionalism led us to very similar conclusions. We argued that the explanation of any action must be given in terms of the end to which that action was directed and the rules relating means and ends employed by the actor, even though the end might not be the end of the actor himself, but the dominating end within a total system of interaction. We should therefore agree with Weber when he says 'Perception of its (an action's) meaningfulness is the presupposition of its becoming an object of investigation', for unless there were some such end to which explanation could be referred we should not attempt an explanation. We should treat the action as mere behaviour. It is only its relationship to the end which makes it a cultural and a social fact.

Moreover we saw in our argument about the formalism of Parsons' approach that the structure of social action was highly variable because the ends of social action were variable and as we said 'rich in content'. Thus instead of sociology being concerned only with the construction of a limited number of models of social structure arising from a limited number of formal value patterns, we said that it should seek to establish patterns as varied as the ends which men seek in association.

Finally we saw that the question of whether a particular social structure was to be explained in terms of an 'integrationist' or a conflict model could only be settled once one knew what the ends of action were. This would also fit in well with Weber's approach in his essay on objectivity.

MANNHEIM AND MYRDAL ON THE PROBLEM OF
OBJECTIVITY IN SOCIOLOGY

The position taken by Karl Mannheim on the question of objectivity is in the same general tradition. Its most noteworthy features are that it takes the side of Dilthey as against Weber on the issue of 'understanding' and that it develops certain implications of Weber's notion of 'relevance for value' in the direction demanded by a theory of social conflict.

Like Weber and Dilthey, Mannheim opposes the positivist approach which seeks to render all social facts measurable and 'unambiguously ascertainable'. He invites us:— 'to think what becomes of our psychic and social world when it is restricted to purely externally measurable relationships', and argues that 'There can no longer be any doubt that no real penetration into social reality is possible through this approach . . . It is clear that a human situation is characterizable only when one has also taken into account those conceptions which the participants have of it, how they experience their tensions in this situation, and how they react to the tensions so conceived.'[1]

This would appear to be achieved by the explanation of action and culture in terms of our conflict model or in terms of Weber's value oriented approach, but Mannheim feels that it is necessary to go right back to Dilthey. He advocates:— 'thas approach which, following Dilthey, I should like to designate as the understanding of the primary interdependence of experience', and argues that,

> In this approach by use of the techniques of understanding the reciprocal functional interpretation of psychic experience and social situations becomes immediately intelligible. We are confronted here with a realm of existence in which the emergence of psychic reations from within becomes evident of necessity and it is comprehensible not merely as an external causality, according to the degree of probability of its frequency.[2]

Yet the actual technique of understanding which Mannheim advocates is much more definitely set out than that of Dilthey. He holds that these are certain terms which are so 'replete with valuations' that only a *participant* in the social system can understand them. Thus it is necessary for the sociologist to enter into social situations as a participant if he is to be able to write significantly about them. This may mean the sacrifice of what is sometimes thought of as the necessary detachment and objectivity of the scientist, but the attempt to achieve objectivity in this sense is a positive obstacle to the attainment of sociological knowledge.

> the purposefully oriented will is the source of the understanding of the situation. In order to work in the social sciences one must participate in the social process, but this participation in collective unconscious striving in no wise signifies that the persons participating in it falsify the facts or see them incorrectly. Indeed, on the

[1] Mannheim, *Ideology and Utopia* (1940), p. 40.
[2] *Ibid.*, p. 40.

161

contrary, participation in the living context of social life is a presupposition of the understanding of the inner nature of his living content. The disregard of qualitative elements and the complete restraint of the will does not constitute objectivity, but is instead the negation of the essential quality of the object.[1]

Now Mannheim would appear to be wrong here for two reasons. The first is that he confuses the psychological question of what arouses the sociologists interest and how he acquires his knowledge with the logical question of the validity of that knowledge. It may well be the case that we can gain insights from participation in the social process, which we would not in fact gain by standing outside. But these insights can be converted into explicit hypotheses capable of being empirically tested. The second reason is that he assumes that in order to include what he calls valuations in our explanations we must grasp the situation in its entirety. But this is by no means the case. As Weber says, 'One does not have to have been Caesar, in order to understand Caesar'. And we might very well construct a model of Caesar's motivation which takes account of the value elements which Mannheim has in mind without grasping every detail of his situation. Once one interprets his behaviour in terms of a voluntaristic theory of action, one must take account of these value elements.

But Mannheim is broadly right in pointing out that in some sense 'the purposively oriented will' is the key to understanding culture and social action. Unless we see behaviour as related to the purposes of the actor we notice only its trivial and irrelevant aspects. And he uses his notion of the necessity of social participation by the sociologist to raise another extremely important point. This is that we only become aware of the ends of our own action when we come into conflict with people whose ends are different. As a psychological observation this is sound and it is of importance in relation to the criterion of selection of problems for investigation. We only become aware that behaviour does present a problem for explanation when we realize that it is related to ends which might be called into question. As Mannheim puts it:—

In personal life, self-control and self-correction develop only when in our originally blind vital forward drive we come upon an

[1] *Ibid.*, p. 42.

162

obstacle which throws us back upon ourselves. In the course of this collision with other possible forms of existence, the peculiarity of our mode of life becomes apparent to us ... We become visible to ourselves, not just vaguely as a knowing subject as such but in a certain role hitherto hidden from us, in a situation inpenetrable to us and with motivations of which we had hitherto not been aware.[1]

But this raises a further point. What Mannheim points out here is that the behaviour of an individual has significance not only in relation to his own ends, or those of his culture, but in relation to other forms of existence with which he comes into collision. Thus whether such behaviour is functional or dysfunctional and whether it will be possible for it to be continued depends upon the point of view from which we look at it. If we regard the actor's own ends or those of his culture as given, then the behaviour might be thought to be functional and necessary. But if the ends with which he comes into collision are given, then the behaviour is dysfunctional and will be stopped.

This is precisely what we said in regard to the ruling-class version of our conflict model. The actions of the subject class or those of the ruling class may be judged from two points of view. Moreover the ruling class will see its own expectations of subject class behaviour as necessary and the subject class will see them as impossible and untenable. Thus there will be not merely two pictures of the world governed by two different sets of ends, but one picture of the world which represents it as a stable, and another which sees it as marked by conflict, contradiction and an inevitable tendency towards change. Hence we should be driven to formulate some such categories as Mannheim does when he talks about ideologies and utopias.

His definitions are as follows:—

The concept ideology reflects the one discovery which emerged from the political conflict, namely that ruling groups can in their thinking become so intensively interest bound to a situation that they are simply no longer able to see certain facts which would undermine their sense of domination. There is implicit in the word 'ideology' the insight that in certain situations the collective unconscious of certain groups obscures the real condition of society both to itself and to others and thereby stabilizes it.

The concept of utopian thinking reflects the opposite discovery of

[1] *Ibid.*, p. 43.

the political struggle, namely that certain oppressed groups are so strongly interested in the destruction and transformation of a given conditions of society that they unwittingly see only those elements in the situation which tend to negate it.[1]

As we said, the ruling class will put forward an ideology which seeks to represent its own position as legitimate. The subject class will put forward a counter-ideology which denies this claim to legitimacy. What Mannheim adds to this is that the ideology will not need to represent the existing situation as legitimate if it can get it accepted that it is scientifically necessary.

Now we are in a position to pose the problem of objectivity in the special way in which it is put by Mannheim. We are faced with two accounts of a social system, one of them ideological and the other utopian. What then are the objective scientific facts of the situation?

Mannheim's conclusions arise from the fact that he regards these ideologies and utopias as valid forms of sociological knowledge. The fact that they rest not upon detached investigation but upon 'the purposely oriented will' strengthens rather than weakens their claim to be regarded in this light. But what are we to make of the fact that their conclusions contradict one another? Mannheim's answer is that social facts do involve contradictions of this sort and that the only way in which we can attain objectivity in sociology is to put the two sets of conclusions together. The truth for the sociologist is the summation of the partial truths of the ideologists and the utopians.

This is hardly a very convincing conclusion and it involves a curiously mechanical way of treating the relation between the ideologies and utopias. But this is because Mannheim sees these ideologies and utopias not as situational elements in themselves, but as sociologies. In fact, if they are treated as situational elements, it would be necessary to go on to show how far either of them was accepted in practice and how far the actual behaviour of the classes was in accordance with their predictions. Behind the ideologies and the utopias there is a balance of power and it is that balance of power which ultimately determines what is objectively true. Mannheim finishes up in a position not unlike that of Parsons. Both concentrate on studying normative and ideological elements and ignore the substructure of power on which such elements rest.

[1] *Ibid.*, p. 36.

There is, however, a second line of argument about how to obtain objectivity in sociology which Mannheim uses and this is perhaps more important. This arises in connection with his proposals for a sociology of knowledge.

The ideologies and utopias mentioned above are not merely produced by the relatively naïve actors in the situation whom we observe. They are also put forward by those who think that they are doing objective sociology. Thus much which passes as sociology is in fact an ideology or utopia which has the effect, if not the purpose, of supporting the existing social system or helping to overthrow it. Mannheim holds that it is the task of the sociologist of knowledge to 'unmask' such sociologists and to show the relationship between their approach to the facts and their social position. By so doing we do not show that their work is worthless, but we show that it is only relatively true. Thus, in addition to supplementing knowledge from one point of view by knowledge from another to gain an objective perspective, we may also gain this perspective by stating openly the value-standpoint of the sociologist who puts it forward.

The same emphasis on making our valuations explicit is made by Myrdal in the appendix to his *An American Dilemma*.[1] Like Mannheim he argues that biases in social science cannot be erased simply by 'keeping to the facts' and by 'refined methods of statistical treatment of data'. And as a justification of his own approach he tells us that:— 'science becomes no better protected against biases by the entirely negative device of refusing to arrange its results for practical and political utilization . . . there are, rather, reasons why the opposite is true.'[2]

Arranging one's results for practical and political utilization means of course showing which institutions and which activities are conducive to which ends. And the task of applied sociology is to start by recognizing some specific ends as given and then going on to show through a normal causal study what factors in the situation are means to its attainment. Clearly this is one task of the sociologist. And it is a task which can be objectively carried out providing that the sociologist does make his value premise explicit and does not pretend that his conclusions are true 'for society'.

Myrdal is less concerned with the problem of pure sociology,

[1] Reprinted in Myrdal, *Value in Social Theory*, p. 119
[2] *Op. cit.*, p. 128–9.

i.e. the sort of sociology which is concerned not with the question of what means are necessary for the attainment of given ends, but with how the social system is likely to develop given the ends, often conflicting, which the observed actors set themselves. But he does appear to be partially concerned with this problem when he discusses the 'relevance' of various value standpoints. As he says:—

> Relevance is determined by the interests and ideals of actual persons and groups of persons. There is thus no need of introducing value premises which are not actually held by anybody.
>
> Within the circle of relevance so determined a still more narrow circle of significance may be taken to denote valuations which are held by substantial groups of people or by small groups with substantial social power.[1]

Thus Myrdal implicitly recognizes that the power at the disposal of various groups in support of their valuations actually determines the outcome in structural terms. And this balance of power can be reasonably objectively determined.

The work of Weber, Mannheim and Myrdal forms a single methodological tradition. What we can learn from it is that systems of social relations are not mere facts, but facts related to a purpose or end. But, since there are many possible ends from which a system can be judged, two consequences follow. (1) That the sociologist may select a special field for investigation, the criterion of relevance being determined by the value standpoints from which he starts. In this case objectivity is achieved by making his value premises explicit. And (2) that the actual course of development of a social system will depend upon the balance of power behind the conflicting ends. In this case the course of development is capable of being relatively objectively determined because the balance of power can be relatively objectively determined. Nonetheless the very notion of a balance of power is meaningless except in relation to groups pursuing conflicting ends and here again such ends must be made explicit.

THE SCIENTIFIC ADEQUACY OF SOCIOLOGICAL EXPLANATIONS

Thus the contention that there are many conflicting value-standpoints from which social facts can be considered does not

[1] *Ibid.*, p. 157.

mean that sociology cannot be objective. But we must now turn to a major preliminary difficulty. This is that our models which relate behaviour to ends in terms of a scheme of action must be proved to be valid before we can use them to explain such behaviour. In Weber's terms, is it possible that our explanations should be not merely adequate on the level of meaning but also causally adequate? This will be the focus of our concern for the remainder of this chapter.

Weber first puts forward the idea of what he calls causal knowledge in his essay on objectivity, immediately after he has emphasised the importance of the value element in explanations.

'Cultural science', he says, 'involves "subjective presuppositions" in so far as it concerns itself only with those components of reality which have some relationship, however indirect to events to which we attach cultural significance. Nonetheless it is entirely causal knowledge exactly in the same sense as the knowledge of significant natural events which have a qualitative character'.[1]

But 'cultural science' is only 'causal knowledge' if certain additional processes are gone through beyond putting forward an ideal type as a hypothesis. All that we have done when we suggest that behaviour is explicable in terms of particular pattern of motivation is to tell a plausible story about it. We feel that we have made sense of it. But we may, of course, be quite wrong. Hence until we have made some sort of test of our hypothesis independently of the data it is used to explain we cannot claim any scientific validity for it. This was the point which Weber wished to make against Dilthey in stressing the need for causally adequate explanations.

Now Dilthey would have maintained that such explanations could not be given because there was no relationship at all between understanding culture patterns and proving causal relations. Relations of meaning and causal relations for him have no connection with one another. A parallel argument has recently been revived by Winch in his book *The Idea of a Social Science*.[2]

Winch uses the parallel which we used in expounding Dilthey's position between understanding a culture and understanding a language. He argues that statistical investigation of

---

[1] Weber, *The Methodology of the Social Sciences*, p. 82.
[2] Winch, *The Idea of a Social Science* (1958).

M

a language could only enable us to solve such problems as how frequently a word occurs, whereas what we wish to know is what the words mean and that this is quite a different matter.

It must be asked, however, whether the parallel between the understanding of a language and the understanding of a culture is as exact as Winch supposes. There is, it is true, a parallel between language and any sort of symbolic activity, but two points may be made about culture in this respect. In the first place, not all cultural activity is of a symbolic sort, and, secondly, that which is does not involve the complex and integrated symbolism of language. Thus it may be the case that both the symbolic and the rationalistic aspects of culture are understandable in something much more like scientific terms.

Clearly it is the case that some activities can be understood as the scientifically appropriate means to the attainment of certain ends. And in the case of the two other sorts of action which we discussed in Chapter Five it is also possible for us to understand the action in a sense quite different from the sense of understanding when we speak of understanding a language. In the one case, that of non-rational action, we say that it is understood when we have shown what the end is and that there are 'ritual rules' for its attainment which lead us to expect action of this sort. In the other case, that of expressive action, we say that the action is explained when it is related to some inward state and to a set of rules setting out the appropriate forms of symbolism for that state.

In each of these cases, then, we have a hypothesis put forward to explain the action which is stated in a form which makes it capable of being empirically tested. To test the explanation of the action as being rational in pursuit of a particular end, we enquire whether the actor does have this particular end in view. To test the second sort of explanation we again seek evidence as to what end the actor was seeking and what rules actually govern his conduct. To test the third type of explanation we should seek evidence as to the inward state of the actor and also evidence as to what sort of symbol was normally used to express such a state in that society.

When we have considered such evidence and our hypotheses are not disconfirmed we are entitled to say that we have given a valid scientific explanation, as much so as any physicist who makes predictions as a result of deductions from his theoretical laws and finds them confirmed. It may have been misleading of Weber to speak of such explanations as 'causally adequate' and to say that his hypotheses could be established by statistical laws based on what happens, but nonetheless there are procedures for empirical testing here which are not logically different from those of natural science.

What seems to worry Winch, however, is that the form of the hypotheses used involves philosophical problems. Thus he criticizes R. S. Lynd's interpretation of West Indian voodoo magic as a 'system of impartially true and reliable causal sequences' and says that the validity of this interpretation cannot be settled by any appeal to statistics. He then goes on:—

> What is needed is a better interpretation not something different in kind. The compatibility of an interpretation with statistics does not prove its validity. Someone who interprets a tribe's magical rites as a form of misplaced scientific activity will not be corrected by statistics about what members of that tribe are likely to do on various kinds of occasion (though this might form part of the argument); what is ultimately required is a philosophical argument . . . [1]

Now it must be admitted that there are philosophical problems involved in the formulation of hypotheses about motivation. It is a philosophic question for instance what it means to have an end and what one means by speaking of means and ends rather than causes and effects. It is a philosophical problem, too, to distinguish between the nature of rational and non-rational action. But equally there are philosophic problems involved in the use of the term 'cause' in natural science. This, however, does not stop scientists from testing causal hypotheses. The point is that, without being able fully to comprehend the nature of 'cause', scientists know that one of its implications is that of involving a recurring connection between phenomena. Equally we need not solve all the philosophical problems involved in the notion of means and ends, or the rules of ritual action to say that they imply a necessary connection between observable phenomena. Then if the connections which were predicted by our hypothesis are found to hold empirically, the hypothesis may be regarded as confirmed.

In the case quoted from R. S. Lynd there are two possibilities.

[1] *Op. cit.*, p. 113.

One is that the magical practices may indeed be explicable in terms of rational action. It could be that, as the functionalists of Malinowski's type say, these practices survive because they fulfil a function quite apart from the intentions or beliefs of the magicians. The sociologist, it should be remembered is not necessarily seeking to explain the practices in terms of the intentions of the magicians themselves, but in terms of their role in a system of interaction. But it is also possible that Lynd has not proceeded in a thorough-going manner to test his hypothesis empirically. If it were so tested, it might be found that the rationalistic ideal type employed was invalid and that another type involving a different logic explained the facts better.

It must be admitted, however, that the systematic analysis of the possible types of action (e.g. rational, non-rational, expressive, etc.) has only just begun in sociology. Thus, although we understand well enough what is meant by rational action, because we use such patterns of action continually in our every-day life, we know little about the logic of, say, religious action. That is why we simply have to accept its rules as arbitrarily given. An essay like Frankfort's *Logic of Mythopoeic Thought*[1] or the work of Levy-Bruhl points the way to what might be done, and it may be that this is the task especially of philosophers. But this does not alter the fact that we can, even without having solved these problems, put forward hypotheses about both rational and non-rational action which lead us to expect particular phenomena, and which may be regarded as confirmed if those phenomena do in fact occur.

Our next problem, however, is the practical one of finding ways of establishing sociological hypotheses and turning them into 'causally adequate' explanations. This is not as simple as it seems because the hypotheses which we have to confirm are not simple patterns of individual motivations as we have rather been suggesting but complex models of developing conflicts or integrated systems such as we discussed in Chapters Six and Seven.

It is worthwhile in the first place to notice the method which Weber used in practice to confirm his hypotheses about the relationship between Calvinism and Capitalism. Having established that there was a meaningful connection between the Calvinist ethic and the spirit of Capitalism he went on to

[1] Frankfort *et al.*, *Before Philosophy*, p. 19.

a number of studies which were, in fact, intended as proofs of the relationship. He showed that capitalism was strongly developed in countries which were Calvinist in religion and very poorly developed in Catholic countries. And he showed that in other civilizations, although there were many other factors present thought to be favourable to the development of capitalism, capitalism had not in fact developed.[1]

What Weber is doing here, clearly, is to use Mills' Methods in a very rough way to prove the relationship. This is a causal proof in the ordinary sense in which causal proofs are made in experimental circumstances or by use of the comparative method. But it is not always possible to use this method both for practical reasons and because of certain limitations which Weber himself imposed on his ideal types.

According to his early essay on objectivity the sort of comparative method which is suggested here ought not to be possible, because in that essay a great deal of emphasis is placed upon the uniqueness of historical events. Weber was opposed to general laws and to the notion of generalized elements which can be found repeated in different combinations from culture to culture. Hence, if the elements involved in the capitalist situation had been ideal typical elements as he first defined them, the sort of proof which he seeks to give in *The Protestant Ethic and the Spirit of Capitalism* would not be possible.

It is necessary to emphasize this, because the sorts of model which we have suggested would be themselves related to particular ends and appropriate only to the analysis of particular social systems. How then, if we cannot appeal to the comparative study of civilisations, can we hope to validate such models? Or does this limitation mean that we would be forever confined to putting forward hypothetical models without ever being able to confirm them?

The danger is that, if we are not able to use the comparative method which rests primarily upon Mills' Method of Difference, we shall simply produce ex post facto analyses of social systems. That is to say that, starting with known facts, we shall simply connect them all up in terms of some plausible hypothesis. If, however, there has been no independent attempt to

---

[1] *See* Parsons, *The Structure of Social Action*, pp. 500–578 for an extended discussion of Weber's proof.

disconfirm such a hypothesis, it can only be a hypothesis and not a scientifically valid explanation.

But there is no reason why our analysis should be entirely ex post facto. The hypotheses which we introduce to explain facts are complex theoretical constructs and they always have empirical implications other than those from which we started. It is always possible to check on these other empirical implications in order to see whether our model does in fact apply. True the logic of such a proof is only that of the Method of Agreement, which is the weakest of Mill's Methods, but this is a step beyond a simple ex post facto analysis which can be tailor-made to fit awkward facts.

Further it should be remembered that the proofs which we give here may be made stronger than a simple proof by the Method of Agreement in two ways. On the one hand the agreement which is shown will not simply be between two phenomena, but between a whole interconnected set of phenomena predicted by the model. And on the other hand, although we set out to devise a model which will explain the uniqueness of the particular society, in fact such a model will have some general elements which make rough comparisons with other social systems possible.

The position appears to be one in which sociology starts off as an interpretative science making ex-post-facto analyses and devising plausible models to explain the facts which are observed. It cannot hope to demonstrate the validity of these models with the precision of natural science, but in the course of arguments proofs which rest on the logic of empirical science are introduced. Such proofs will consist of pointing to facts not previously considered in the original situation which would fit in with predictions in terms of the model and of rough comparisons with systems explicable in terms of similar models.

One point should be noted about Weber's notion of ideal types, however, which if we were to accept it, would make such proofs logically impossible. This is his idea that the types represent limiting cases only, or that they involve 'a one-sided accentuation of one or more points of view'. This could mean, if taken to extremes, that the types were a kind of caricature, and one cannot in fact prove a caricature, because one knows in advance that in any particular case the elements of the caricature will not be there in a pure form.

It must be doubted whether there is in fact complete consistency between Weber's definition of ideal types and his demand for 'causal' proof as it is presented in his argument against Dilthey. What use ideal types defined as limiting cases and 'one-sided accentuations' have is in providing illuminating *interpretations* of social facts rather than in supplying valid scientific explanations. A book like Veblen's *Theory of the Leisure Class*[1] is a good example of work of this kind. Its value lies in providing a preliminary orientation to the study of American culture. But it cannot, taken by itself, yield proveable hypotheses about that culture.

Of course, if Weber had argued that his ideal types were simply theoretical abstractions, which could be applied to empirical fact only if preceded by a ceteris paribus clause, they could be regarded as a source of valid explanations. Taken together with other factors they could explain observed events. But Weber always insists that they are not abstract in this sense but refer to 'concretely possible' cases. He does seem, in fact, to be trying to get the best of the empirical and the theoretical worlds in his definitions and hence the logical status of his ideal types remains obscure.

The possibility that the ideal types might perhaps be regarded as theoretical abstractions, however, raises a final important question. If they did refer to elementary theoretical components of social systems it might be possible to construct out of such elements a general theory of social systems, any particular social system being regarded as explicable as a particular sort of interaction of the variables. This does seem to be one direction in which sociology could develop, and Parsons especially has gone beyond Weber in this way.

But our own discussion of theoretical models for the analysis of social system leads in the opposite direction. Our emphasis upon the study of the ends of such systems is in line with Weber's insistence on the principle of relevance for value. In practice the goal of sociological research will always be the understanding of a structure in relation to the ends which it serves, and though general elements may emerge from such studies and there is a case for codifying them, the primary focus of interest will remain the understanding of a particular society.

It is possible, of course, that even studies of this kind may

[1] Veblen, *Theory of the Leisure Class* (1934).

involve a process of theoretical abstraction and that the actual course of development may be explained in terms of the interaction between analytically separable abstract elements. But these separable elements are not abstract in the sense of not being related to a particular situation. They are elements of that situation looked at separately from one another. Our model of a class situation involved abstractions of this kind when we analyzed the structure of each class and its goals separately. But the goals were specific to a particular society and the abstract classes were ultimately seen as interacting with one another in a particular conflict situation.

The goal of a science of sociology, then, according to the view taken here is the discovery of *valid* models for the interpretation of behaviour in social systems. By valid models we mean models which have in some way been subjected to the test of disconfirmation. This is the real importance of Weber's insistence upon explanations which are adequate on the level of meaning and also causally adequate. It is right to emphasize as Mannheim, Myrdal and Weber have done that the starting point for the construction of models is to be found in value-premises, and that there are many such starting-points possible. But ultimately the test of the validity of a model is the same as that for any theoretical model used in empirical science. It must be shown to be capable of correctly predicting empirical events.

One final point may, perhaps, be made. The actual evidence in terms of which we confirm or disconfirm our models may be of a quantitative or a qualitative character. In principle we should prefer it to be quantitative. But quantitative evidence is of little use if it is not evidence about the problem in which we are specifically interested. We should by all means welcome any attempt to devise exact methods of observation of relevant data. But we do not need to say that because there is no evidence of this quantitative kind, that sociology is completely unscientific. Its claim to scientific status would be justified in terms of its theoretical clarity and its honest attempt to prove its theories by empirical testing. Sociology will probably never be an exact science, in the sense which physics is, but nonetheless there will always be great value in attempting to introduce into sociological discourse the disciplines of science on a theoretical and an observational level.

X

CONCLUSIONS:
THE SCOPE OF SOCIOLOGY

SUMMARY OF CONCLUSIONS

THE aim of this book has been to emphasize the importance of sociological theory in research and to discuss in general terms some of the problems which continually recur in any attempt to construct a sociological theory. We are now in a position to review the conclusions which we have reached and to suggest what the problems are, with which a theoretically-oriented sociology is competent to deal.

(i) The Role of Theory in Sociology

In each of the first three chapters we emphasized the important role which theory had to play in sociological research. In the first chapter we showed that, whatever the conception of science held by the sociologist, careful consideration of the methods of investigation proposed in terms of that conception showed that some sort of theoretical construction was necessary. In the second chapter we reviewed some of the major fields of sociological research in which an empiricist or historicist approach had been predominant. In these cases we argued that either the conclusions reached were not necessarily sociologically relevant conclusions, or that the conclusions, although sociologically relevant, were unclear, because terms referring to social facts were ill-defined. In the third chapter we showed that the field of sociological study could not be settled by some sort of ostensive definition but required the development of a special theoretical frame of reference in terms of which data which were

175

common to sociology and other sciences could be studied. Here we drew attention to the important fact that such entities as social relations which seemed to be the basic data of sociology, were not simple observable entities but theoretical constructs used to explain observed behaviour.

To emphasize the role of theory in this way, particularly perhaps in Great Britain, is to run the risk of being accused of advocating 'system building' or what is sometimes called 'arm-chair theorizing'. It must be emphasized therefore that the object of the sort of conceptual analysis and theorizing which we have been advocating is to make empirical research both more exact and more free from concealed value judgements than much research which claims to stick to the empirical facts is at present. One particular point to be noticed is that if basic terms like 'relation', 'role' and 'action' are not carefully analyzed on a theoretical level they cannot be operationally defined. That is to say that it is not clear what sort of evidence would be looked for to confirm or falsify statements which use these terms. Thus the object of theorizing is not to turn away from empirical fact but to make truly scientific research into empirical facts possible.

(ii) Action, Conflict, and Anomie

The point of attention of our theorizing in the third chapter was to define the subject matter of sociology. First of all we considered Durkheim's attempt to demarcate the social as that which was external to the individual actor in a situation. We saw that, in fact, this attempt ended in theoretical obscurity and that Durkheim himself had eventually recognized that society can exist only in and through the individual. We then proceeded to an analysis of the concept of a social relation and saw that the principal empirical implication of this term was that the parties to a social relation had 'expectations' of each other's conduct. This in turn raised the question of whether these expectations were valid or not. Amongst the reasons why they should be regarded as valid we listed such factors as the existence of shared norms requiring conduct along the lines of the expectations, the sanctions supporting these norms, and the desire of the parties to win and retain each other's approval.

On the other hand we noticed at this stage in the argument a point which was to become a major theme in later theoretical chapters. This was that the case in which the expectations of a social relationship were completely justified was a limiting case only. Actual social relations were seen to depart from this pure type in two directions. On the one hand there were cases in which there was inadequate communication or understanding between the parties. This we called the case of anomie. On the other hand there was the case of conflict, in which the parties understood each other well enough, but because their ends were in conflict with one another they could not fulfil each other's expectations.

It is worthwhile at this point to add something about the relation of these two concepts, 'anomie' and 'conflict', because it is the former concept which has predominated in recent theoretical writings which have considered deviations from the pure type of the completely institutionalized relationship, whereas in this book it is the notion of conflict which has been made central. We have not sought to deny that there are social situations characterized by anomie in this strict sense. But we would maintain that they represent a very special field of study and that the concept of anomie has been generalized in an unwarranted way to cover cases of conflict. This has led to an inadequate conceptualization of the problem of conflict and to distortions which have some ideological importance.

Thus, for example, as we noticed in a later chapter, Durkheim treats class conflict as an anomic form of the division of labour, rather than a central structural feature of capitalist society, with the implication that the conflict could be resolved by agreement on values. Similarly one finds that the doctrine that 'strikes are due to misunderstanding' has great prevalence in modern industrial sociology. We should say that it would be more profitable at least to examine whether strikes could not be understood as a case of social conflict. Or yet again one finds Merton's writings of *Social Structure and Anomie* instead of *Social Structure and Social Conflict*, although he clearly shows that in American society large groups of people explicitly reject in whole or in part the ethos of their society.

When we turned to the functionalist approach of Radcliffe Brown, we saw that the failure to conceptualize social facts adequately, and the resort to an analogy instead of a relevant and clearly defined theory, was a means whereby the elements of both conflict and anomie were excluded from discussion.

Functionalism, as we showed, led inevitably to an 'integrationist' model of society, in which activities, if they were regarded as explained at all, were explained in terms of the need to maintain the social structure.

In criticizing this approach we pointed out that 'need' was a teleological term which required special justification when applied to social structures. We found, however, that when we attempted to understand what was meant by social structure, that it depended upon the interests, needs, aspirations or values of individuals and groups. And since there might well be conflicts in these, the further attempt to elucidate the meaning of the term structure, inevitably meant that the integrationist assumptions of functionalism were called into question.

The types of Social Action and Interaction. From this point on we concentrated on discussing social structure in terms of human action. But action itself is not a simple notion and it was necessary for us to look at some length at the various possible types of action and the way in which elementary unit acts were united with one another in means-ends chains and in social systems.

The central problem relating to types of unit acts was the conceptualization of non-rational action. Our discussion of this was by no means exhaustive, but we noted three important cases. The first was irrational rather than strictly non-rational action. In this case the actor could be thought of as essentially trying to be rational but failing either because of misinformation or bad logic. The second case was that in which the actor did not pretend to be rational, but either sought an end for which there were no scientifically appropriate means or sought to attain his ends through procedures prescribed by non-scientific 'ritual rules'. The third case was that in which it seemed artificial to speak of ends and means at all. In this case we spoke of expressing an inward state through an appropriate symbol, the appropriateness being defined in terms of a scientifically arbitrary set of rules.

Sociology, however, is not concerned with action, as such, but with social interaction, and it was then necessary to go on to show the way in which the behaviour of other parties became involved in sequence of action. They were involved, we saw, as means and conditions in the original actor's pattern of motivation. At this point it was possible to distinguish between psychological and sociological explanations. The former could be thought of as explanations of an actor's action in terms of his own pattern of motivation, whereas the latter must be thought of as explanations of one actor's actions in terms of the requirements of the pattern of motivation of another. Hence the mystery of the externality of social facts disappeared. From the point of view of the actor whose actions are being explained the social determinants of his behaviour are external. But they are not external to all individuals.

It is convenient to discuss sociological theory on this microcosmic level, but here we noticed that this analysis of the elementary case of social interaction was intended as a means of exposing the essentials of large and complex systems of interaction. A picture of such a large and complex system of interaction could be built up on the basis of the recognition that just as A's action demanded the co-operation of B, so is B's action demanded that of C, C's that of D, and so on indefinitely. Thus the employment of the action frame of reference does not lead to an 'individualistic' sociology, but is quite compatible with the recognition of complex social systems which are internally integrated.

Nonetheless it is a mistake to assume that the only form of sociological analysis on the macrocosmic level is that which assumes total integration. Thus we could not accept Davis' analysis of the controlling institutions of social systems as implying that acceptance of the normative control of these institutions was inevitable in society. Instead we noted them as being concerned with problem areas of interaction. There would be a property problem, a power problem, an ultimate value problem and a religious problem in any society. In the case of an integrated society this would mean a property system, a state enjoying 'legitimate' authority in terms of ultimate values, and a shared set of religious beliefs and practices. But in a system involving conflict it would mean conflicts over ownership, political conflicts, disagreement of values and a variety of religious faiths.

The sixth chapter was concerned to clarify the relationship of the sort of sociological theory outlined here to that which has been developed by Talcott Parsons. Parsons we saw first as reacting against utilitarianism and positivism and demanding the recognition of normatively governed action in social systems. But this seemed to have led him to an undue emphasis upon these normative integrating elements taken in abstraction from the context of interests and power in which they operated. Secondly we showed that Parsons explicitly concentrated in his microcosmic analysis of interaction on the special case of a completely institutionalized social relation. And thirdly we questioned the formalism of his analysis of the collectivity-integrative elements in social systems, arguing that the crucial point at which societies were integrated or divided was to be found in the ends sought by groups.

(iii) The Theory of Social Conflict

Thus we proceeded while retaining the action frame of reference to an analysis of situations of social conflict. In the first place we noted that even a functionalist theory could be made more realistic if it recognized that at some points normative controls rested on, and were in delicate balance with, a dynamic power situation. We were able to agree with a great deal of Coser's analysis of this problem. But much more we were concerned with the understanding of situations based upon really disruptive conflicts based upon disagreement not over intermediate norms but over the ends to which the activity of the social system taken as a whole should be directed.

Now no functionalist theory can deal with these problems. We therefore put forward an alternative theory of conflict situations, the development of conflict groups and the possible relations between them. It is not necessary to repeat in any detail here what has been said about the nature of that model. But there is this one point to be made. This is that whereas functionalism can give no account at all of conflict situations, our model can be used to explain in an alternative and rather more convincing way many of the phenomena which are taken by the functionalist to be signs of social integration.

In the first place it should be noted that the alternative which we propose does not take us back to Hobbes' war of all against all, the point from which Parsons started. It assumes the existence of a very large measure of social co-operation on each side of the conflict situation taken separately. In the analysis of conflict-group formation all that we said about sociological as distinct from individual psychological determinants of behaviour in Chapter Five is very relevant. The formation of a conflict-group is a special case of the development of a complex interaction system such as we discussed there.

But much more important is what we had to say about the relations between the conflict-groups in what we called the ruling-class situation. Obviously the relations of a subject class to its rulers can cover a considerable possible range. It may engage in open revolution or in passive defiance, it may accommodate to the situation or it may find itself struggling to maintain the loyalty of its members in the face of the ideological assaults of the ruling class. In all these cases the situation is one of conflict and they all include elements which could not be explained by the integrationist type of model. However in the last mentioned case we have a point at which this sort of model and our own do offer rival explanations.

In our view the sort of normative agreement which comes to exist between the members of different classes is best explained in terms of the concept of legitimacy. This was a concept which was introduced into sociology by Max Weber and it is an extraordinarily well chosen one. It is introduced by Weber into his theory as one of the possible bases of *imperative co-ordination*. It is not introduced as arising from any sort of consensus of norms. Moreover it is defined purely in terms of the subjective attitude of those who accept the legitimacy of an order. Weber gives three reasons for accepting the legitimacy of an order, but he in no way excludes the possibility that the claim to legitimate authority might be rejected and explicitly states the possibility that imperative co-ordination might be accepted on other grounds.

The value of this concept rests on the fact that from the beginning it brings the normative system of a society into relation with the balance of power between the co-ordinators and the co-ordinated. The special case of normative consensus thus appears as the end point of a scale at which the claim to legitimacy is fully accepted. But at the other end of the scale there would be the case where counter-norms were proposed by the subject groups and where the attempt to rule by legitimate authority was replaced by rule by violence.

To state the problem of normative order in this way also leaves scope within our theory for the notion of the 'engineering of consent'. There clearly is a very important difference

181

especially in mass societies between the acceptance and internalization of an order proposed by the ruling class on the one hand and the case in which consent is obtained by manipulation of the sentiments of the subject group. The sort of model of a ruling class situation which we have suggested allows for all these alternative possibilities, whereas the integrationist model allows only one sort of basis for co-operation.

On the other hand the recognition of the balance of power as the variable upon which the existence of a ruling-class situation rests opens up other possibilities. A change in the balance of power might push the total situation not merely beyond the acceptance of the legitimate authority of the rulers, but beyond any sort of accommodation to their rule. Then the two possibilities of a total revolution or of a negotiated compromise are opened up. Thus we should be led to an analysis of the elements involved in the balance of power on the one hand and of the variety of possible sorts of accommodation, revolution and compromise on the other. A whole range of problems in contemporary society are illuminated by the model and the variable elements which deserve investigation immediately become clear.

Thus we would suggest that the reshaping of sociological theory, so that it is built around the notions of conflict, imperative co-ordination and the balance of power, would make it far more applicable to the analysis and understanding of the central problems of the recent social history of industrial societies. For when one considers the nature of this history, it is hard to credit that sociological theory could have remained so closely tied to the concept of integration and consensus.

Take, for instance, the case of the development of secondary education in Britain. According to the functionalist view, such education would be necessary not merely to transmit the more difficult skills required by an advancing technology, but also to transmit the norms and values of the society. But any study of the debates which proceeded the introduction of the Education Act of 1902 will show how various were the pressures which were actually at work. Some sections of the ruling classes were opposed to the idea of secondary education altogether. Those who were in favour of it vied with another about controlling it, because they had different ideas about the content of education. And the working-class demanded it either in the hope that their children would 'get on' in the existing order, or because they recognized that such education would help them in the establishment of a new social system. The resulting educational system was the outcome of a compromise between these conflicting pressures. It is not a system which could in any way be explained in terms of orthodox functionalist theory. But the manner of its development and the eventual compromise is exactly what we would have expected in terms of our conflict model.

(iv) The Theory of Conflict and Marxist Sociology

This might be interpreted as a plea for looking at social history and the sociology of contemporary society in terms of the 'class struggle' which was central to Marx's sociological thinking, and it may, therefore, be worthwhile to say something here about the relevance of Marxism to contemporary sociology.

In the first place we should note that Marxism is inhibited by the Hegelian tradition and the Hegelian terminology within which it had to work. Thus the terms and concepts which it uses (e.g. terms like 'dialectic' and 'alienation') are not particularly clear in their sociological meaning. But on the other hand there are times, as in the Theses on Feuerbach when Marx seems to have a very clear grasp indeed of some of the problems which we have been led to formulate in writing about social systems in terms of action. And above all, in recognizing that conflict was of the essence of social systems, Marxism kept alive an approach to sociology which was badly needed as the emphasis of theoretical thinking moved to the study of 'normative elements' and 'consensuses'.

When one turns to the special field of interest of Marxist sociology, however (i.e. the study of social class), one finds that some sort of revision of Marxist positions is necessary. This is not, as we saw, because the Marxist type of theory has to be replaced by a status theory such as that advanced by Lloyd Warner, but because concepts like 'relation to the means of production' and 'a class-for-itself' turn out to be considerably more complex than Marxists often imagine them to be. What we did in our chapter on class was first to look at the problems of the Marxist-type theory and the Warner-type theory separately and then to show how these problems could be resolved in terms of our general model of social conflict and in terms of Weber's notions of 'meaning' and 'legitimacy'. The problems could be resolved in this way because neither the model of a completely revolutionary situation, nor that of 'government by consent' is appropriate to the conditions which we were considering. The mistake, however, is to suppose that every society must be of one type or the other. The model which we suggested is one which would lead us to expect a society marked by profound ideological conflict and its members perplexed by problems of class loyalty.

(v) Validating Propositions about Conflict Situations

Looking at societies in this way raises issues of a methodological kind. Thus in the last chapter we were not merely seeking, having put forward a theoretical model to ask how it could be validated. The nature of the model determined the way in which methodological questions arose. As we saw in our discussion of Weber's notion of relevance for value, of Manhneim's conceptions of ideology and utopia and of Myrdal's emphasis upon value premises, it is possible to look at social systems one-sidedly. Indeed since the necessity of social structures depends upon the necessity of the ends which they serve it is essential that at some stage they should be looked at in this way. But this does not mean that objectivity is impossible. For apart from the ends or value premises which we make explicit as being 'given' all that we say in these terms is capable of and subject to empirical verification.

The emphasis which we have placed on 'ends', however, led us to agree with Weber's conception of sociology as concerned with the explanation of particular historical situations, rather than seeking to verify general laws about social systems by the comparative study of different social systems. The general model of conflict which we have propounded is not a general theory of social systems in this sense. It is merely a guide for the formulation of particular models applicable to particular social systems. It is these particular models which have to be proved and tested by comparing their predictions about various sorts of social activity with the actual course of events. A general theory of social systems could only be established if it could be shown that there were recurring elements in the ends which were sought through various social systems.

THE TASKS OF SOCIOLOGY

The tasks which are presented to sociology are of a two-fold character. On the one hand there is the need to establish a valid model for the analysis of a particular social system which he is studying. And on the other hand, once such a model is established he may be faced with explaining some partial and particularized form of behaviour in terms of the part it plays in the total system. However, in any particular research situation there will be a choice as to what shall be regarded as a total system, that is what the scale of our interest should be, or what segment of the total system we should study.

(i) The Analysis of Small-Scale Systems of Interaction

In some studies we may decide that we will ignore the problem of the role played by a particular group, institution or relation within a larger social system. For instance it is possible to study a factory without relating it to the overall picture of the relation between the classes, or to study a youth club, a family or a marriage without reference to the function of socialization which these agencies fulfil for a class or a society. In these cases the factory, youth club, family or marriage will be regarded as a system in itself.

When we say it will be regarded as a system in itself, however, we do not imply that the model to be used is an 'integrationist' one. It may be that there may be a greater element of consent by one party to the expectations of another in small-scale situations like this, and it is obvious that the sanctions employed to enforce compliance will be very much less drastic than they are in the kind of overall conflict which we have been discussing. But it is equally obvious that to study a marriage without recognizing the possible elements of conflict and balance of power, a youth club without recognizing the possibility of conflict between the expectations of the members and what the club-leader provides, or a factory without recognizing the strains imposed by the collective bargaining, would be to leave out the dynamic element in the situation. To understand such situations means to grasp the way in which the prevailing relationships and norms rest upon the balance of interests and the balance of sanctions between the different parties.

Thus we may assume that many sociologists will continue to

185

study small-scale interaction systems taken out of their total context and studied as objects of interest in themselves. And it may well be that such studies may be related to particular value interests of the participants or the observer. In this case the object would be to discover the particular situational elements which existed and did not exist in cases when the desired state of affairs was attained and when it was not. In small-scale studies of this type there are a sufficient number of similar situations for comparative studies to be made.

Here, however, it is necessary to repeat Myrdal's warning that such value-oriented studies are only truly scientific if the value standpoints from which they begin are made explicit. For instance a great many studies of marital stability, and instability are based upon the assumption that marriage as a life-long union is desirable. But, as Goode[1] shows, in his penetrating study of post-divorce adjustment it is perfectly possible to study broken marriages from the point of view of the adjustment to separation of the parties. Similarly in the notorious case of industrial sociology it is too often assumed that the object is to discover how harmony between employers and employees may be promoted, when such studies might equally well take as their starting point the demand of the employees for a higher standard of living. But there is no reason why anybody should not study the best ways of achieving marital stability or industrial harmony, so long as he makes clear what he is doing.

But though, for practical reasons, much sociological research will continue to be confined to small-scale specialist studies of this kind, such studies will always be subject to severe limitations so long as the influence coming to bear on the objects of their study from outside are ignored. Thus community studies, for example, are somewhat artificial if they ignore the fact that the community is subject to the influence of the values disseminated by the mass media of communication on a national scale or the fact that its members are affiliated to nation-wide organizations of economic and other kinds. Or again the study of religious groups or political parties tend to be purely formal in character, unless the relevance of their activity in the extra-religious extra-political world is taken into account. Thus it is vitally important that large-scale studies of

[1] Goode, *After Divorce* (1956).

the interrelationship between institutions on a nation-wide or civilization-wide basis should be made. And it is at this point that the sort of overall model of the total system of social interaction which we have been considering is of importance, at least as a means of preliminary orientation.

(ii) The Significance of the Study of Class Conflict

The starting-point for such a model must always be a study of the ends to which the system as a whole is directed. It may be that in some few societies we shall find that these ends form a unitary system. But the usual case will be that in which there some sort of conflict of ends and hence some sort of group or class-conflict. Thus the study of class-conflict in all its manifold complexity will always play a central part in the development of sociological studies. Such a study is not on the same level as the study of specialized economic, political, religious and other institutions. It is an essential preliminary to any of them. This is so, even if the sort of picture which Dahrendorf paints of class-conflict as localized in separate institutions in industrial society is true. If this is the case, then the fact that it is is one which should be understood by any student of the specialized institutions. The study of class conflict must in any case be placed at the centre of sociology because what the sociologist of class conflict is doing is to concern himself with the general model in terms of which all the institutions of the society are to be looked at.

If a conflict model is adopted, whether Dahrendorf's or our own, this makes a significant difference to studies of the separate institutions. Instead of having a determinate structure they appear as areas in which there is a particular sort of conflict of values and aspirations. In fact it might be argued that the term 'institutions' is a misleading one because it seems to suggest a greater measure of organizational stability than is in fact the case. It may be better therefore not to speak of institutional studies but rather of the problem areas of social interaction.

(iii) The Main Areas of Institutional Analysis

This being said, we should have no further quarrel with the sort of classification of the problem areas which is made by Davis or Parsons or Malinowski. Clearly every society has a problem of allocating facilities, a problem of distributing power and a problem of values. And with regard to the last mentioned clearly there is a problem not merely of expressing and maintaining values but of transmitting them. So there is that whole area of problems concerned with 'socialization' which has received little attention here, but which is an important part of any systematic study of social systems.

We have already mentioned that one object of the study of these problem areas is to study the internal organization of the social systems to be found there. What we have to emphasize now is the study of the interrelations between the institutions. Much of the work which has been of most lasting value in sociology has been in this area. Weber's study of the relations between Calvinism and Capitalism is the outstanding example.

But we should not assume in advance that all specialized activities are knit together into a single integrated system. It is true that as against Coser, we insisted that they should not be regarded as varying at random to one another. But one of the implications of our conflict model is that the sort of compromise which is achieved on one front may differ from that achieved on another. Hence one might expect that say, the educational system and the economic system might be dysfunctionally related to one another because the ruling class has made concessions on one front and not on the other. If we remember the principle that the value premises or ends from which an institution is studied should be made explicit, there is no reason why such dysfunctional relationship should not be scientifically demonstrated. We should show that the educational system is as it is because it has been determined by one set of ends and that the economic system is as it is, because it has been determined by other ends.

(iv) Relevance and Irrelevance for Value

Hence our conception of social research is of separate studies going on in a number of fields which will be determined by the relevance for value for the individual. Broadly speaking the two sets of value interest which have predominated in practice are an interest in problems of personal adjustment (e.g. the interest of the social worker) and an interest in political affairs. But as the volume of studies grows the possibility of a tighter relationship between these two areas emerges. This could not be better put than it has been by Wright Mills.

188

The sociological imagination enables its possessor to understand the larger historical scene in terms of its meaning for the inner life and external career of a variety of individuals. It enables him to take into account how individuals, in the welter of their daily experience, often become falsely conscious of their social positions. Within that welter the framework of modern society is sought, and within that welter the psychologies of men and women are formulated. By such means the personal awareness of individuals is focused on explicit troubles and the indifference publics is transformed into involvement with public issues.[1]

But this tighter relationship is not to be sought necessarily in an abstract general sociology theory or, as Radcliffe Brown used to suggest in a 'natural science of societies'.[2] Nor can it be found by way of the 'middle principles' suggested by Merton.[3] What is required is an attempt to relate particular specialized problems to some sort of theoretical model of the total system of interaction of which they form a part. An overall theoretical model of the particular society which he is studying is an essential tool if he is to see particular problems in perspective. Given continued argument about the general nature of the social system which we are studying, particular problems, even of a personal kind, take on new meaning and real sociological significance.

Finally it may be asked what sorts of research are excluded by our approach to sociology. The answer is all kinds of research to which the special training of a sociologist can bring no special illumination. It is no answer to this to say that the research involves a high degree of mathematical exactness. If mathematical exactness were the main requirement of social research, then sociology would best be left to the mathematicians.

Thus research into what Weber called the 'life chances' of human beings strictly speaking forms no part of sociology. True it poses a problem for the sociologist who asks whether the differential distribution of life-chances is indicative of a particular power system or whether it means the emergence of segregated ways of life. But by itself it is simply a part of the study of human biology in which exact descriptive and mathematical techniques have been developed to a high level.

[1] C. Wright Mills, *The Sociological Imagination*, p. 5.
[2] *See* Radcliffe Brown, *A Natural Science of Society* (1957).
[3] Merton, *Social Theory and Social Structure*. Introduction.

Nor would we include as *necessarily* sociological all those many studies which prove statistical correlations between aspects of human behaviour and a variety of causes. Again such studies pose sociological problems, but they only become sociological in themselves when the correlations are explained in terms of some sort of theory of social interaction.

The fact that such studies are carried out for the most morally worthy of reasons does not make them a part of sociology. What sociology has to do is to try to introduce the disciplines of scientific thinking into the debate about a very special set of determinants of human behaviour which has gone on without much scientific discipline from the beginnings of the history of mankind. What this book has been concerned to do is to explore the nature of these determinants and to discuss the special problems raised by any attempt to apply scientific discipline to them.

INDEX

191